SRI RAMAKRISHNA AND HIS DISCIPLES

SRI RAMAKRISHNA AND HIS DISCIPLES

BY

SISTER DEVAMATA

GYAN

Published by

Gyan Publishing House
5, Ansari Road
Daryaganj, New Delhi-110002
Phone: 011-47034999, 9811692060
E-mail: books@gyanbooks.com

Distribution Network
gyanbooks.com
India, USA, Canada, UK, Australia

ISBN: 978-93-6433-156-2 (PB)
First Published, 1928

2nd Impression 2024

Printed at: Gyan Press, Delhi.

SRI RAMAKRISHNA AND HIS DISCIPLES
Author: SISTER DEVAMATA

SRI RAMAKRISHNA
AND HIS DISCIPLES

SRI RAMAKRISHNA
AND HIS DISCIPLES

BY SISTER DEVAMATA

Author of "Days in an Indian Monastery," "Building of Character," "What is Death," etc.

ANANDA - ASHRAMA

LA CRESCENTA, CALIFORNIA

In Humble Tribute

FOREWORD

East and West are but two points on the horizon and as we extend our vision these two apparently distant points come closer and closer until they blend in unity. When the eye of the Occident is turned upon the mysterious East, as it is so generally termed, often it is dazzled, perplexed and confused by the endless variety it finds; and this usually results in gross misconception regarding the true import of the Eastern soul.

In order to know the heart of the East, one must be willing not merely to look on the surface, but to gain an insight into the deeper instincts of the human soul. Therefore, whenever there is a sincere attempt to know the life, the habits, the faith of the more ancient world of culture and its great teachers who have created that culture, it must meet a welcome from all thinkers and believers in larger unity.

We may travel and travel and always we travel among strangers; but when our sight of understanding is unfolded, then no matter how far and how distant the place, how seemingly different the civilization, always we find ourselves among our fellow-beings and kinsmen. When one touches the life of the far East with the hand of love and sincerity, it produces a note of harmony which must ever convince us that the true heart of the East and the true heart of the West are made of one substance, that we cannot love one without loving the other.

The author of this remarkable record of one of India's lofty Spiritual Lights had rare opportunities to gather material for her task and she possesses an equally rare gift of being able to lend to her portrayal exceptional beauty of literary form. Her picture is a true one and is drawn with great delicacy of feeling. Her knowledge came to her first hand and it leaves a profound impression on the heart and life. The present volume cannot fail to bring about a better understanding of India and a broader sympathy for humanity at large.

PARAMANANDA.

AUTHOR'S FOREWORD

It is with faltering confidence and deep humbleness of spirit that I begin this volume on Sri Ramakrishna and the great ones whom he gathered round him. Much has been written of him, much is being written, further record seems scarcely justified. Yet I find justification for my undertaking in these words spoken to me by the disciple Sasi who later bore the Master's name: "We might talk of Ramakrishna for days and days together and still he would rise up before us as absolutely new. So unfathomable is he!"

Each one who attempts to portray Sri Ramakrishna merely uncovers one more facet of his nature. Always there remain others unrevealed. So it is I add my tribute.

Further and more fundamental reason for so doing is given by the same disciple. When I was leaving Madras, the disciple Sasi said to me: "Come back in a year and we will write a life of Sri Ramakrishna." I did not return and the disciple Sasi passed away, but he left in my keeping a rare store of material. He had talked unceasingly of his Master. What he said I wrote down each day as opportunity offered. He read the written words and declared them to be his own. His sanction lent to them new value.

I had thought to publish these notes by themselves. That, however, would have left me an unused accumulation of incidents and facts related to me by others; also a large measure of my own association with the disciples would have remained untold.

My purpose in the following pages is not to present an exhaustive record of a life but to give a vivid picture of a remarkable personality. To mass around it a multiplicity of facts and incidents would be to obscure it. A great spiritual Light such as was Sri Ramakrishna has no need of fact or legend to exalt him. He himself is greater than his life, greater than his words.

Out of fullness of devout feeling and richness of blessing I turn now to my task, with the prayer in my heart that I may prove adequate to its lofty requirement.

DEVAMATA.

ANANDA-ASHRAMA,
LA CRESCENTA, CALIFORNIA,
FEBRUARY, 1928.

CONTENTS

INTRODUCTORY NOTE

What I have told in these pages came to me from many sources,—from the widowed wife, from the immediate disciples and from householder devotees, with all of whom I was closely associated in India. The chief source from which I have drawn was the disciple Sasi. Whenever there was any divergence in the detail of the narrative, I kept to his version. He was in intimate contact with Sri Ramakrishna, the memory of the Master permeated his every thought, hence there seemed no surer authority to follow.

Sri Ramakrishna is spoken of in various ways. His name is Ramakrishna. *Sri* is a term signifying "revered." His disciples, most of them, speak of him as *Gurumaharaj*, "great Master." The women disciples call him *Thakur*, "Lord." The general public during his life knew him as the *Paramahamsa* or "illumined soul" of Dakshineswar. I have retained these different descriptive names in order not to destroy the color values of the portrayal.

For the same reason I have used the boyhood names of the immediate disciples. Sri Ramakrishna knew them by no others. A list of their religious names is given at the back of the volume. Also a glossary is provided. To preserve the local color I have been forced at times to make use of foreign words, but I have tried to reduce the number to a minimum and when possible to define them in immediate sequence.

AUTHOR.

SRI RAMAKRISHNA
AND HIS DISCIPLES

CHILDHOOD

Sri Ramakrishna was always a child even after he had grown to manhood. Only a child-nature could harbor such utter simplicity, such purity and guilelessness as were his. "He always had his Divine Mother beside him. This you must remember," the disciple Sasi once said to me. "Just as a baby of two or three months has a loving mother always beside it to look after it and provide its needs, so his Divine Mother was always by his side. Whatever he wanted he asked for and She, being all-powerful and all-loving, at once brought him that."

How he came into this world is of minor importance. It has seemed to me always that too much stress is laid on the manner of birth of great Manifestations; too much of faith and dogma is made to rest upon it. All nature is a miracle. Trees and birds and flowers and sunshine make constant festival. Each act of creation has its hymn of joy; and mighty souls need no extraneous circumstance to glorify them. They are glorified by their own inherent super-earthly glory. The fact and legend which gather round their nativity are but the expressions of man's cumulative marvelling at further miracle in an unbroken sequence of miracles.

One condition, however, is essential for the working of the new wonder,—those who bring the child to birth must stand very close to the dividing line between divine and human. No others would be worthy to serve as channels for the embodiment of divinity. Sri Ramakrishna's parents fulfilled this requirement fully. Although wholly unaware of it, for twenty years they were making themselves ready. Their preparation began really the day they rumbled along a country road in a rude springless bullock cart, with their scant worldly possessions stowed away behind them under a loosely stretched canvas hood.

They were moving from their native village of Dereypore to the adjacent village of Kamarpukur in Bengal. Their fortune had been swept away. A rich landowner of the neighborhood had called upon Khudiram, Sri Ramakrishna's father, to give false testimony in a law-suit and Khudiram had refused. The landlord in vengeance had involved him in a long and intricate legal controversy, which had sapped Khudiram's resources and left the family ruined. A friend in the neighboring village had offered them a small cottage and an outlying rice field. Here in his thirty-ninth year Khudiram began a new life with his wife, Chandramani, a son of ten and a little girl of four.

There was no bitterness or complaint in their hearts, but the rude blow had severed all attachment to material advantage. Khudiram arranged a Shrine in the garden of his home and spent his days in prayer, meditation and study of the Scriptures, unmoved by the harsh reproach of neighbors incensed that, while still in active years, he should give up all effort to retrieve his losses.

His ardor of spirit was shown one day when he was going to pay a visit to a member of his family who lived fourteen miles away. He had walked nearly the whole distance when he saw by the roadside a Bel tree in fresh leaf. These new leaves of the Bel tree were specially pleasing to the form of Deity he worshipped. He climbed the tree eagerly, picked some of the leaves and hurried home to lay them in the Shrine while they were still fresh and green. All thought of his errand and the long way he had travelled was blotted from his mind by the joy of finding an auspicious offering for his Lord. This earnestness of devotion gradually silenced all criticism and won for Khudiram such reverence that, it is said, when he passed along the village street, people would rise and stand in respectful salutation.

Chandra also was content in her humble home with its thatch of palm leaves, its walls of sunbaked mud and its two dimly lighted rooms within. There was only food enough for one meal a day and not infrequently she gave that away to an unexpected guest or a passing mendicant and went about her tasks in joyous fasting. So purged was her mind of all desire that, the story is told, once when a friend on his way to a fair, asked her what he could bring her, she declared she had not a single need. Then seeing his disappointment, she said quickly: "A few hairpins I could use."

Sometimes she was left alone with the children while her husband went on pilgrimage. The last of these pilgrimages took place when Khudiram was sixty years old. Despite his age he made the entire journey on foot undaunted by sun, dust and distance. His body was quickened by the devout fervor of his mood. He was going not for himself but to free a soul bound to earth yet longing to be free. The thought of releasing this earthbound spirit who had made appeal to him added to his ardor. When he reached Gaya, glowing with eager joy, he hastened to carry his offerings to the Shrine and bow down before the sacred footprint in the stone. As he rose, he beheld a group of shining figures with one more radiant than the rest whom he recognized as Sri Krishna by the peacock's feathers on his head.

Later when he was sleeping in his lodging this being appeared to him again and told him that he would take fleshly form in his house. Khudiram might have grown proud and boastful that he had been chosen for so high a mission; but he thought only of the One who stood before him and he cried out in lowly protest: "Lord we are not worthy. Our little house is too small and bare of comfort. We could not serve you well enough. Choose those who can give you better care."

During her husband's absence visions had come also to Chandra. They culminated one day when she paid a visit to the Temple. As she entered the Temple, the sacred image in the Shrine suddenly became a living flame moving in advancing circles until it enveloped her and she fell down unconscious on the Temple paving. They lifted her and carried her to her house. When she awoke, she found in her heart a new sense of sanctity and dedication, as if something holy and apart had taken life within her. She told her experience to Khudiram on his return and he told her his. They both realized that a great call had sounded for them. In profound humility they responded.

Khudiram returned to his study and worship. Chandra took up again her homely tasks; but there was about her now an added loveliness and sweetness, a keener joy in self-sacrifice and service. As the hour for her delivery approached she grew anxious lest travail might seize her before the day's duties were finished and the offering for the Lord made ready, for there was no one else to prepare it. Her husband rebuked her gently, saying the child she carried was no ordinary one and would not fail to come at the proper moment. The waiting mother was able to complete all her tasks. Then taking with her a woman of the village, she went to a little hut in the garden and there in the stillness of the dawn a son was born to her.

The year was 1836. The child was given the name of Gadadhar. In the stories told of him by the villagers it is difficult to sift fact from legend, but there can be no doubt that his babyhood and childhood were unusual. The disciple Sasi spoke to me of it in these words: "Sri Ramakrishna's life was so peculiar that many things, if told, would be regarded as mere stories. He knew from the beginning why he had come and he began teaching from the time of his birth. Even as a baby and later wherever he was, those about him always recognized that there was something strange and unusual about him, something divine.

"When he was only three or four years old, he was walking through the fields one day, carrying like all the little boys a small basket of fried grains. The sky was very blue and across it flew a flock of white herons. These herons fly in flocks of fifty or one hundred and as they go they form the most beautiful garland across the sky. As Gadadhar saw it, he was suddenly reminded of Sri Krishna with a garland of flowers about his neck and he fell down in *Samadhi*.

"Later when he was about six years of age and was going to school, he used to read out of *Sisubodha*—a book which begins with the alphabet and has in its pages a little of every branch of learning, among other things a number of stories from the Ramayana, the Mahabharata and Puranas, not always grammatical in their language but told simply and graphically. This Gadadhar would read aloud to the women neighbors, less lettered than he: and as they sat in a group listening, a wild black monkey would come down from a tree overhead and sit clasping his leg. Then as soon as the reading was over, up it would go. No one knew whence it came or where it went. But it never failed to come with the others.

"The villagers loved him and he mingled freely with them all. When it came time for him to be invested with the holy thread and be initiated into the rites of the religion of a Brahmin, according to the custom he was told to choose some lady in the village from whom he should beg first. As a Brahmin it was his duty to select one of his own caste. Instead, however, Gadadhar chose a poor blacksmith's widow named Dhani as his godmother, because although of low caste she was noted for her piety and purity of character. The family objected strongly to his choice, but he held to it firmly. He was always quick to recognize merit wherever it was to be found. When his family refused to accept Dhani as his godmother, he shut himself up in his room and did not take meals for a whole day, until his eldest brother, Ramkumar, finally promised to let him have his own way."

Gadadhar's mood was most often gay and playful, even mischievous. He was fond of hovering near the bathing-ghat and teasing the elderly ladies who after their morning bath sat on the bank counting their beads or performing their devotions. He would sing and dance round them with an innocent smile on his face. Then when they scolded him, he would run away laughing, only to come back and begin again. At last the ladies appealed to his mother and a word from her checked him.

Sometimes he would disguise himself as a little girl and even his girl playmates could not detect who it was. Thus dressed, he would play tricks on them and tease them, but no one could get really cross with him or scold him very hard. An irresistible charm enveloped him which disarmed and conquered. There was no wound or sting in his fun. It was always harmless and called forth laughter, not tears. Even the elderly ladies by the bathing-ghat loved him.

A dark shadow fell over his life, however, and his laughter turned to sadness. When he was eight years old his father died. It brought bitter grief to all the family. Gadadhar felt it keenly. He grew grave and thoughtful. The sorrow came just before he received the holy thread and his mind was already turning into more serious channels. His mother was stricken by her loss. The widow's unbordered cloth became for her a cloister veil. The world slipped from her. Her life grew even more conventual and austere. She gave herself up to meditation, prayer and worship in the modest household Shrine.

Gadadhar helped her in her household duties and in the worship. Many profound questions rose in his mind. It seemed the beginning of a new and graver life. The disciple Sasi, in speaking of this time, related to me these incidents: "During the funeral ceremonies it is a custom in Bengal to invite the learned men of the surrounding places to a big meeting hall to hold discussions on religious subjects. Once when such a meeting was held in the mansion of the Laha family, Gadadhar talked with the *Sadhus* in such a way that they all admired and blessed him, saying: 'This extraordinary child will turn out to be an extraordinary man.'

"He was looked upon as precocious and promising by almost all the people of the village, some of whom used to regard him as more than human. One illiterate shell-cutter, by name Chinu (Srinivasa) used to take him to some solitary place and worship him with flowers and other offerings; and the simple man actually used to weep before him in true devotion. By this we can understand the influence which unconsciously he exercised around him in his boyhood.

"Once his mother gave him a new cloth. The family was so poor that the purchase of a cloth for any of its members was no small matter. Gadadhar put on the new cloth and went to see some wandering *Sadhus* who were stopping at a house in the village. Listening to their conversation such *Vairagyam* (renunciation) seized him, that he tore his new cloth, tied a strip of it about his little thighs and came running home to his mother, crying out with his face all aglow: 'See, mother, I am a *Sannyasin* now!'

"When he was about twelve years old a band of strolling players came to the village. But they had no Siva. The man who played the part had fallen ill on the way. At that time Gadadhar was a little stout and his fine appearance made them ask him to take the part. But when he came on the stage the consciousness of Siva so filled his mind that tears began to trickle down his face and he fell down in *Samadhi.* People thought that he had been seized with a fit and at once the performance stopped."

Many itinerant players passed through the village, pausing on their way to give a performance or two. Gadadhar was always keen to see them and so remarkable was his memory that afterwards he was able to stage a play he had witnessed, remembering words and songs and action and teaching them to his comrades with extraordinary exactitude. More often he preferred to compose his own plays on the spur of the moment. They were acted in a mango grove on the outskirts of the village with his playmates as the actors. His favorite subject was Sri Krishna at Vrindavan; but he never allotted the part of Sri Krishna to himself, although the other boys urged him to take it. He invariably chose the part of Radha. It was sweeter to him to worship than to be worshipped. So was it throughout his life.

Most of the children with whom he played were very poor and their daily meal was coarse and scant. He longed to give them something good to eat, but he too had little. He thought and thought how he could do it and finally an inspiration came to him. He got some clay, moulded it into sacred images, dried and colored them and set them up on a stand in the market place. They were so well modelled and had so much of charm and grace about them that soon they were all sold and he was able to give a grand feast to his comrades. It seemed a forecast of his later custom.

STRUGGLE

Sri Ramakrishna was not wholly unlettered, as some have represented him in their zealous desire to bring into higher light his later power and wisdom. He did not touch the university and his schooling was not extended, but he read aloud to his village neighbors and I have held in my hand a book which contained his writing. That he cared little for text-books and study was due to the innate swiftness and depth of his own thought processes. The printed page was too slow a medium of knowledge. He knew the fact before he had finished studying about it. Mere book learning in itself had little value for him. He reached out for that which stood behind.

When he was sixteen years of age, he went from his village to Calcutta that he might continue his studies at the Sanskrit College which his eldest brother had established there. The brother was a learned scholar and bore bravely the burden of the family's maintenance. The second brother seemed to have little practical resourcefulness and succeeded poorly in his attempts at earning. The elder sister was married. There was also a younger sister.

Gadadhar was not only to study, he was to help his brother also in the school. It is said that one day as he sat on the school verandah a Brahmin boy came up the verandah steps with some fruits and small coin in his hand. Gadadhar asked him where he had got them. The boy explained that he had been performing some priestly ceremony for a neighboring family. "Is that all your years of schooling have done for you?" Gadadhar exclaimed in questioning rebellion and he closed his book. The bondage of learning held him no more. "Let me know God's thought first, then I shall be content to know what man thinks," he cried out.

In later years he put the same thought thus: "First let man know his infinity, then let him play with the finite. Let him seek God first, then the world." The disciple Sasi in repeating to me these words added, as if still speaking for his Master: "Let God shine alone in His glory. Now too often we let the ego shine above Him and we throw God into the background. We make Him the last consideration. We seek matter first and spirit afterwards. Reverse the process."

Gadadhar's sudden and unbending resolution to study no more brought grave perplexity to Ramkumar's mind. He had deep respect for scholarship and he was counting on his brother becoming a teacher and contributing his share towards the support of the family. The boy must not remain idle and the question rose "What could he do?" Ramkumar was serving as priest in a Temple on the Ganges six miles above Calcutta. Sometimes Gadadhar accompanied him when he went to perform the daily worship. Mathura Babu, the son-in-law of the Temple's founder, saw him there more than once and felt strongly drawn to him. Finally he proposed that Gadadhar become Ramkumar's assistant. Ramkumar was delighted with the plan but it met with unexpected opposition from Gadadhar himself.

The Temple of Dakshineswar was a new one, built as a votive offering by Rani Rashmani, a widow of large wealth but of lowly station. She belonged to the Sudra or serving caste and many sternly conservative Brahmins for that reason refused to serve in the Temple. Ramkumar, more liberal and tolerant, had accepted the position of officiating priest, but Gadadhar now refused with great decisiveness. It was not caste prejudice that impelled him. If he could have been swayed by that, he would not have chosen the blacksmith's widow, Dhani, to be his god-mother when he took the sacred thread. It was something far deeper of which at the moment he may not have been consciously aware.

His special message was that of unbounded tolerance and universality. It was the Vedic message: "Truth is one, men call it by different names." Or to translate it into his own words: "Various are the roads that lead to the House of the Lord. Every religion is only one of many paths that lead to God." He himself was free from bias but he had no quarrel with the conservative. It is easy enough to break the tradition of one's own faith and through sheer indifference to manifest a lukewarm tolerance towards other forms of faith; but to remain staunch and ardent in one's own religion, yet to see and acknowledge equal power and sanctity in other religions—that is true catholicity.

Such catholicity Sri Ramakrishna embodied. "Being firm in devotion to your own chosen Ideal, do not despise other Ideals; but honor all." These words define his attitude. An orthodox Brahmin, he was careful in all religious tradition and observance; at the same time he possessed the largeness of thought and feeling of the most emancipated free-thinker. His care in caste and tradition was an intuitive, perhaps unconscious, preparation for his later task.

His gentle wisdom even at this early period is apparent in this passing incident. While cleaning the Temple Shrine one day the sacred image was dropped and a leg broken. The accident called forth great confusion of opinion. Some wished to discard the image; others, to mend it. They asked Sri Ramakrishna and his reply was characteristic. A certain tenderness of love gathers round the image which is worshipped day after day. For the devout mind even the symbol of divinity has a heart-throb. It seems pulsing and alive. Sri Ramakrishna felt this and answered: "When a son breaks his leg, the mother does not throw him away."

An insistent yearning was beating within him. Gradually it overcame his opposition and he became a priest in the Temple of the Great Mother of the Universe. "At first he was strongly opposed to undertaking the duties of priest," the disciple Sasi told me, "but when he at last consented, his whole soul went into the service of the Mother. At daybreak he would be in the garden picking the most beautiful flowers for Her. He would prepare the most fragrant bath, roll the most delicious betel leaves, do everything for Her with the whole devotion of his heart."

He rose at four, brought water from the Ganges, strung garlands to adorn the holy image, rubbed the sandal paste on the stone, set out the camphor, prepared the lights and made all ready for the day's worship. It was not a lifeless form he served but a living Presence. His ardor infused it with life. That is the purpose of all forms of worship. They counterbalance the concrete, dominating reality of material things by creating a concrete spiritual reality. They lend convincing vividness to the inner verities and lead step by step "from unreal to real, from darkness to light, from the dying to the undying." I quote the words of an ancient Sanskrit prayer.

It matters not what form we take. It may seem even puerile and childish to the skeptic or the cynic, but if it brings light where there was darkness, joy where there was sadness, Divine reality where there was blankness, a sense of companionship where there was loneliness, it should have our reverence and be given a place in the world's ritual. Sri Ramakrishna found room for every phase of devotional expression. Not one was excluded or condemned. "Bow down and worship where others kneel," was his injunction. "As out of one gold, ornaments of various forms are made; so it is the same God that is worshipped by different nations under different names and different forms."

Warmth of zeal made him tireless and punctilious in the performance of each priestly task. But the very fervor of his worship gradually kindled in his heart a flame which consumed all regard for fixed form and ceremonial. He forgot the order of his Service. Sometimes he waved the burning camphor or smoking incense for long hours without pause; or, feeling the living Presence within himself, he placed the flower, not at the feet of the sacred image, but on his own head. At other moments, driven by inner questioning, he would sink into deep meditation and cease to worship altogether.

Such behavior was an offense against Temple tradition and priestly decorum. All the other Brahmin servers in the Temple joined in outraged protest. Even Ramkumar was at a loss to excuse it. Only Rani Rashmani and Mathura Babu seemed to understand and when all said the boy was mad and must be sent away, they maintained it was a madness of Divine ardor and he must not go. Complete freedom was to be given him and his nephew, Hriday, was to act as his substitute whenever he wished to be relieved from his priestly duties.

He sat no longer at the feet of the Great Mother in the Shrine, but beneath a wide-branched banyan tree on the Ganges side. This banyan was interlaced with four others in such close leafage that it formed a twilight-shadowed grove. Under the tree was a brick platform rising in broad steps. On the topmost step beneath a massive branch just there where it joined the tree, Sri Ramakrishna took his place. Afterwards the branch bent down and covered the spot, setting it apart for all time and marking it as holy.

Here the struggle for ultimate attainment began. Already in the Temple he had been assailed by grave, doubting thoughts. Day after day he had questioned within himself "What is this moulded image? What lies behind it? Is there a living, breathing Universal Mother who watches over Her striving, seeking children? Where is She? Why does She not manifest Herself?" Now on that upper seat under the banyan tree these questions rose again with tormenting insistence.

Body and bodily needs were forgotten. He did not sleep. He did not eat. He scarcely drank. At rare intervals Hriday, the nephew, would pour a little milk between his lips and by striking him on the shoulders would force him to swallow it; or again, at the evening hour when the priest waved the lights in the twelve Shrines along the river bank, the ringing of the bell would call him back to outward sights and sounds. Then in agony of grief and waiting he would beat his brow against the ground and ask the Mother why She had not come.

Perhaps there lingered in his heart some remnant of caste pride that kept Her from him? He would root it out. Swifter than the thought, with throbbing impatience he hurried, almost running, through the gate in the Temple wall and along the shaded road to a neighboring hamlet of low-caste toilers. In India there exists a tradition that if a Brahmin goes to a Pariah's house, the house will burn through excess of honor. It was not easy for the young priest, therefore, to enter such a house; but he watched until he saw a scavenger leave his hut on his unseemly errand, then he went in and cleaned his outhouse. He made himself the scavenger of a scavenger. No vestige of caste prejudice could survive so drastic a remedy. Pride must be dead. Still the Mother did not come.

Further days and nights of fevered inward searching! Then the thought sprang up in Ramakrishna's mind that it was greed of gold that held her back. He went to the edge of the river and taking some Ganges mud in one hand and coin in the other, he made of his hands a balance. Mud was the heavier; why should it weigh lighter then in the measure of our desire? He reasoned:

"What does mud give us? It gives us food. Without it no food would grow. What does gold give us? It buys us food. But unless food is grown, it cannot be bought. Mud then is the more essential. Why cherish gold and scorn the mud? We do not cling to mud, why cling to gold?" With complete detachment he threw both into the Ganges.

Practical minds will say, why did he not keep the gold and use it to some beneficial end. If he had, his reasoning would not have been final. Equality of values would not have been reached. Would he have offered mud to a poor man? So entirely was he weaned from love of money that from that time, it is said, if one touched his body with a coin even when he slept, his muscles would recoil automatically. Greed was gone. Still the Mother did not come.

More days and weeks of questioning and striving. Then the thought rose: Perhaps it was lust of the flesh that made him unworthy of Her Presence. For this fault he knew no remedy; so he sat by the water's edge and wept and wept so bitterly that others came and wept with him. He called and called and called again until the Mother heard and purged him of all desire. But She did not come.

Months went by. The storm of yearning grew and grew. The agony heightened. There was no further word, no motion, scarcely a breath to tell that there was life. The search had gone to the uttermost depths. Then the storm-cloud that veiled his soul broke and through the widening rift there shot a resplendent light. The Mother stood before him, tender, radiant, encompassing. At that moment Ramakrishna became for all eternity a child, the child of the Universal Mother.

ATTAINMENT

The Mother had come. Not a vision, seen with closed eyes; a living Mother with gentle smile and protecting arms; a shining effulgent Presence, yet tender and enfolding. Doubt was gone. Peace had come in Sri Ramakrishna's heart, but no word of triumphant attainment burst from his lips. He spoke to the radiant form before him as simply as a nestling little one might speak to its earthly mother. "I am only a little child," he said. "I cannot care for myself. Who will care for me?" He asked the question; but he knew humbly in his heart that henceforth only the Great Mother of the Universe could give him care and shielding.

Struggle was over, not effort. Much labor lay before him. The rigor of preparation for his mission stretched out through long years. His message was an all-inclusive one. Before he could proclaim it, he must relate his new attainment to every aspiration of the human heart, to every form of religious faith and feeling. To do this he must make acquaintance first with his own inner being. He began the most arduous spiritual practice. The severest exercises in Yoga were tried and mastered.

"He practised *Pranayama* (breath control) so much that he formed a habit of remaining for long periods without breathing," the disciple Sasi told me. "Now and then he would stop breathing entirely. Even after we came to him, he used to tell us: 'Whenever you see that I am not breathing, please remind me.' Sometimes when he was sleeping, we would see that the breath had stopped, then we would wake him up and tell him: 'Master, you are not breathing.' 'Oh, thank you!' he would say and again begin to breathe."

Not hours, but whole days and nights were spent in continuous meditation. Some one asked the disciple Sasi in my hearing if his Master had not remained once for three days wholly unconscious of outer things. His reply was:

"Three days? For twelve years. Through that time he did not know when the sun rose or when it set; he did not know whether he had taken food or not. Occasionally when a moment's consciousness would come, he would feel as if some one was dwelling inside and he would ask: "Who are you? Why are you here?" So completely had the Mother possessed him!

"His body was especially manufactured to stand the shock of these manifestations. It was not an ordinary body. He used to say: 'If one-millionth part of the emotion I feel should come to an ordinary man, his body would break to pieces; just as when a mad bull gets into a garden, it tears and uproots everything there.' He would compare his religious devotion to a mad elephant.

"His mind was so constantly turned towards God that even when he was eating, he would often not be conscious of it and some one would have to tell him when he had eaten enough. 'Have I taken enough?' he would ask; and if the person said 'Yes,' then at once he would stop. Once none of his own was with him and when he asked some other man who happened to be there: 'Have I had enough?' and the man replied: 'Yes,' he said: 'Very well, I will not take any more.' Just then Hriday came in and seeing that Gurumaharaj had taken only one-half the usual quantity of food, he insisted on his eating more. Gurumaharaj then perceived that he was still feeling hungry, but he said: 'No, I have said I would eat no more and I cannot break my word.' "

Sri Ramakrishna felt the need of a more hidden spot for his spiritual practices. On the high platform beneath the banyan tree he was too much in public gaze; so he and Hriday built a little hut under the shadow of a wide-reaching branch not far away and planted a hedge about it with a creeper, which wound itself through overhanging foliage and roof-thatch in such tangled profusion that the tiny hut was completely veiled from inquisitive eyes. But the Temple cows ate up both hedge and creeper and it became necessary to construct a fence of bamboo poles. When materials were lacking for the building of this, Sri Ramakrishna prayed to his Divine Mother and the flood tide, receding, laid on the riverbank a bundle of poles with strong cord and a sharp knife. His prayers were never fruitless.

Later, desiring still greater seclusion, he sought shelter under a Bel tree concealed within an uncleared jungle of brambles and thick undergrowth in the far corner of the Temple compound. One morning he could not be found. Those who watched over his needs looked and looked for him, but in vain. They decided at last that he had begun to meditate on the tidal wall beside the Ganges and, losing outer consciousness, had fallen into the river. Great was their grief and distress of mind. A Temple cow chanced to go astray that same day and the gardener searched for it also without avail. Toward the evening hour, when it was time for the milking, he plunged into the deserted jungle near the garden wall. There under the Bel tree sat Sri Ramakrishna in deep meditation. He had been meditating the whole day. The lost cow too was not far away.

Mathura Babu watched Sri Ramakrishna's growing ecstasy sometimes with reverence, sometimes with questioning wonder. He doubted and believed at the same time, but always he was held spell-bound by the Master's super-earthly simplicity and super-earthly power. When Mathura doubted he would argue boldly with Ramakrishna, as the Master himself related long after to his disciples:—

"Once Mathura said to me that even God was forced to obey His own laws. When He had made them, He could not unmake them. I replied that what God had done, He could undo; what He had made, He could unmake; or He could change one law into another. Mathura asked, 'Can He make a bush that produces only red flowers bear white ones?' 'He can,' I answered. At the moment Mathura did not believe me; but the following day I saw in the garden an hibiscus bush covered with deep red blossoms. There was just one stalk on which beside the red flower was a snowy white one. I picked both on the stem and showed them to Mathura. Then he believed."

At another time when Sri Ramakrishna was reading a hymn in the Temple, he was so overwhelmed by a sense of the infinitude of Deity that he burst into a flood of tears. Seeing him weeping thus, people thought he was undoubtedly mad and wanted to take him out of the Temple. At that moment Mathura Babu entered and forbade any one to touch him. Sri Ramakrishna remained unaware of everything but God for a long time. When he emerged from his state of divine abstraction and saw Mathura Babu standing beside him, he asked like a frightened child: "Have I done anything wrong?" "No, Bhagavan," Mathura replied, "I am standing here merely to guard you."

A stauncher guardian even than Mathura Babu was Rani Rashmani, the builder of the Temple. She never wavered in her faith in Sri Ramakrishna's super-human wisdom and greatness. She sustained and protected him in all that he did.

No show of apparent madness, no eccentricity of behavior ever shook her loyalty. Sri Ramakrishna had the deepest respect and loving regard for her exceptional qualities, but he did nothing to win her favor. When she offended against her higher nature, he was as direct and uncompromising in his rebuke as if she had been the most insignificant Temple servant.

One day when she was performing her devotions in the Shrine of the Mother, she let her thoughts wander away to her worldly concerns. With the penetrating intuition which uncovered every mind to his inner gaze, he perceived what she was thinking and struck her a quick sharp blow on the shoulder to recall her to herself. She took the correction humbly and brought her thought back to her devotions; but Hriday, seeing it, was frightened, fearing that he and his uncle both might lose their positions at the Temple.

Rani Rashmani passed away in February, 1861, leaving Mathura Babu sole executor of her estate. Mathura's first thought was to place the vast resources at Sri Ramakrishna's disposal. He even wanted to convey to him a large property. At the suggestion Sri Ramakrishna grew indignant and exclaimed: "Do you want to turn me into a worldly man?" He received the costly presents Mathura offered him in the same protesting mood. Once Mathura laid at his feet a very beautiful shawl. Sri Ramakrishna took delight in its beauty and wrapped it round him; but when Hriday reminded his uncle that much had been paid for the shawl and he should take good care of it, wearing it only on important occasions, Sri Ramakrishna replied: "Shall I let this miserable shawl take my mind from God?" And he held a corner of it in the fire. "Now it is burned and has no value," he exclaimed with satisfied content; "I can wear it in peace, without fear of greed or pride."

MARRIAGE

It was in 1855 that Sri Ramakrishna accepted the office of priest at the Temple of Dakshineswar. A year later came the first blinding flash of illumination, plunging him into a God-madness which fevered his whole system and changed his entire habit of life. There was no respite or lessening of this madness until suddenly, in 1858, Sri Ramakrishna returned to his native village of Kamarpukur.

The eldest brother, Ramkumar, had died and the second brother, Rameswar, was living with Chandra, the mother, in their village home. Distressing reports of the youngest son had reached them from the Temple. There seemed little doubt that his mind had been unbalanced through excess of religious fervor. No other excuse or explanation could be found for his strange behavior. Chandra's heart ached with anxiety and grief. She devoted much time to praying in the Temple and she fasted and worshipped with increasing devout intensity in the little garden Shrine at home. Finally she determined to send to her son an insistent request to return to his village.

Sri Ramakrishna came at once, but his coming brought Chandra little comfort. She found him changed and sadly unlike the boy who had left her six years before to go to his brother's *Tol* (school) at Calcutta. He seemed utterly detached from family, friends and the world. Human concerns did not touch him. He was indifferent to all outward interests. He shunned companionship. Finding more unbroken solitude in the cremation ground than elsewhere, he chose that as his favorite resort and passed his time there lost in meditation, remaining often far into the night. Even his brother feared to go and call him.

The neighbors began to whisper among themselves that he was obsessed of an alien spirit. These whisperings reached Chandra's ears and awakened a new disquietude within her. She summoned one who was wise in such disorders, but when he tried to exorcise the spirit, a voice was heard saying: "Your son is not possessed by any spirit, nor is he suffering from any malady in either body or mind." This soothed the mother's agony of soul and she became still more hopeful as with the passing of the months she saw her son grow more normal. Little by little he regained his quietness of mind and somewhat of his early boyish gaiety. His old habit of neighborliness returned and he aided his mother in her daily household tasks.

Chandra did not feel secure, however. Something must be done to render the recovery permanent. She consulted with her elder son and they decided they would apply a drastic and final remedy,—they would marry Sri Ramakrishna. At once they set out to find a suitable wife for him, but it was by no means easy. Their poverty was a great obstacle and Ramakrishna's religious madness was not a secret. They grew more and more discomfited. Day after day they looked in vain. Sri Ramakrishna observed the darkening shadow on their faces. Finally he asked what troubled them and they confessed their hidden intention.

They expected rebellious protest. Instead, they met ready acquiescence. "Go to Jayramvati and to the house of Ram Chandra Mukhopadhyaya," Ramakrishna said. "There you will find the little girl who is to be my wife." Some one was dispatched at once to the village of Jayramvati and, returning, reported that the parents consented willingly to the marriage; but their daughter, Saradamani, was only a child of five. Sri Ramakrishna was then twenty-three. Chandra was disturbed on hearing the girl's age and agreed to the marriage reluctantly.

The wedding was perforce a simple one; the family resources admitted of no elaboration of ceremonial or gifts. That the little bride might not be without ornaments during the marriage rites, rich neighbors of Kamarpukur lent their family jewels. The rites over, these had to be returned, but Saradamani clung to her ornaments. She liked their bright sparkle and color. She thought them her own. To take them from her would have meant a storm of child-tears, so Sri Ramakrishna waited until she had fallen asleep, then he removed them so gently that he did not rouse her. The tears came just the same at her waking.

Very different was her later attitude of mind, as is shown by this incident told me by the little bride herself after she had grown to saintly womanhood and was known to the world as "Holy Mother":—

"Thakur (Sri Ramakrishna) had many Mawari disciples," she said, "and in August and September they used to bring him great quantities of rice, *dal* and other stores. One day one of them came with three thousand Rupees sewed up in a pillow and offered them to Thakur. 'I do not want them,' Thakur exclaimed. 'What should I do with them? Take them to Mother.' He brought the money to me and Thakur came with him. As if to test me, he said: 'Why not take the money and buy yourself jewels and ornaments which you have never had?' 'But what should I do with jewels and ornaments? I do not want them,' I replied; and the man had to take his money away with him."

Sri Ramakrishna's marriage was in reality never more than a betrothal and vowed the child-wife to lifelong widowhood. After she had attained maturity, many friends and neighbors expressed unconcealed disapproval of the husband's ascetic course and more than one asked him: "Why do you not live with your wife, have children and do as other sensible Brahmins do?" His answer was: "If I had children of my own, inevitably I should love them more than others. I wish to feel that all the children of the world are my children and that I love all equally."

At another time he said: "If a man once becomes a householder, he can no longer have his whole mind for God. When he is married one-half of his mind goes towards his wife; when children are born the other half goes to his children. Where is there any part left for God?" The disciple Sasi often told me: "Gurumaharaj always made a very great distinction between his householder disciples and his *Sannyasin* disciples. He used to tell us there was a wide gulf between us. I praise the householders, he would say, because they are able to think on God even now and then in the midst of their worldly concerns."

Why did Sri Ramakrishna marry then? There was a profound reason for it. In Indian religious tradition marriage is one of the ten acts of purification which a Brahmin must perform before he can become a teacher of men. Sri Ramakrishna himself explained: "One can become a true *Acharya* (teacher) only when one has passed through all these acts." He who is to guide the human heart must understand every phase of human experience and its relation to the sacramental life of spirit. There must be no omissions in the fulfillment of his religious duty. Only from the root of undeviating loyalty to the requirements of Vedic teaching and custom could come the flower and fruit of Sri Ramakrishna's later universal sympathy and tolerance.

The Indian attitude towards marriage is very different from that of the Occident. It is not a question of individual choice or personal pleasure. It is a social obligation which the great majority of the members of human society owe to the human race. It must not be entered into lightly through momentary attraction or caprice, nor should it be broken lightly. It must be regarded and treated as a vital, lasting, sacramental relation. That is why certain of the Vedic Scriptures deal in such detail with the association of husband and wife—a part of their text often misunderstood and misinterpreted by Occidental scholars.

Though the marriage relation is sacred, however, it must not monopolize. A man, because of it, must not forget his wider responsibilities as part of the larger social body. That would be false to the Indian ideal of marriage. The entire structure of Indian society is founded on the subordination of the lesser to the greater. Uncompromising self-sacrifice is its practical organic basis. The individual must give way to the family, the family must give way to the community, the community to the state and no claim must count against the claim of God.

Human life, according to the Indian or Vedic conception, is divided into four stages, each with its initiating sacrament. Birth and some form of baptism mark the beginning of childhood or the first stage. The receiving of the Holy Word or *Upadesham* opens the door to *Brahmacharya,* student life or the second stage. The rite of marriage initiates into the householder's life or third stage; and *Sannyas,* the act of renouncing, forms the sacramental initiation into the final stage, the forest life. The advancing soul, whether in one earth existence or many, must pass through these four stages. Sri Ramakrishna touched the first three lightly. The fourth absorbed and consumed him.

Sarada Devi never complained of her wifely lot, nor did she feel it a hard one. She lived for many years in the home of her parents and it seemed often as if her husband had forgotten her, so lost did he become at times in religious ecstasy. But when at rare intervals she saw him in his mother's home at Kamarpukur or in her father's house at Jayramvati, he was always gently mindful of her welfare and tried never to cast any shadow over her young heart. Holy Mother later when speaking of this told me the following incident:

"Once I and one of the ladies of my family were eager to go to see the performance of some strolling players, but Thakur would not let us go. When he saw how disappointed we were, he was greatly concerned to console us. He himself acted out a play he had once seen, giving the words, the music, the songs, everything, although he had heard it only once. We were so carried away by his performance that we forgot all about the one we had missed."

He taught and trained his young wife with watchful solicitude and wrapped her about with tender prayer. As the years went by, she grew to be more and more a vital part of his lofty mission and the blessing and privilege of such spiritual association far outweighed any joy that might have come from an earthly relationship.

Nor was she childless. She had countless devoted children who looked to her for comfort and counsel. Many lived near her and came daily to her. There were young men in Calcutta who never went to their office or counting-room without going first to receive her blessing on their day's task. In later years her family was numberless. Sri Ramakrishna often said to her: "When one has earthly children sometimes they are bad and disobedient, but the children I have brought to you are good and pure and will never cause you trouble."

TAKING SANNYAS

Sri Ramakrishna remained in his village for a little more than a year and a half after his marriage; then he returned to Dakshineswar and resumed his priestly office. He appeared to be entirely restored. Scarcely had he begun to worship in the Temple once again, however, when the old madness seized him, more acute, more absorbing than before. In passionate God-yearning, he passed through every degree in the rising scale of devotional ardor. "Men weep floods of tears for the sake of wife or children or for money, but who weeps for God? Yet they complain that they have prayed so hard and still the Lord has not come," he exclaimed to his young disciples later.

He himself wept for God with his whole heart and his tears of devotion carried him to the heights of *Prema*—that state of Divine union in which the devotee is said to become speechless and dazed "through excess of light." The fire of his fervor consumed him, even his body burned with it and he sought relief by standing in the cooling waters of the Ganges for hours together. Various remedies for the scorching fever were tried and found ineffective. At last relief came by rubbing sandal-wood paste on the body and by wearing certain flowers.

At another time his insatiable hunger for God translated itself into insatiable hunger for food. No matter how much he ate the body cried for more. As he had given always little thought to food, the condition seemed inexplicable. His unnatural appetite was appeased finally, not by eating, but by surrounding him with large quantities of savory dishes. The sight and aroma of the food seemed to satisfy him and the abnormal craving subsided. In both these instances the cure was suggested by a *Brahmani* or Brahmin lady who appeared unexpectedly at the Temple and became Sri Ramakrishna's first teacher. Her name was Yogeswari, but she was known always as the *Brahmani*.

One morning as Sri Ramakrishna was gathering flowers for worship in the Temple garden, a boat drew up at the smaller *Ghat* and a lady stepped out on the river-swept landing. She was dressed in the orange cloth of the *Sannyasini*, her feet were bare, her long hair hung down her back and a noble beauty marked both her face and her figure. As soon as Sri Ramakrishna saw her, he left the garden, called his nephew Hriday and told him to request the *Sannyasini* to come to him. She showed no surprise when Hriday delivered the message, but came at once. On entering the room where Sri Ramakrishna was waiting, she cried out: "Baba, are you here? I have been searching for you up and down the Ganges for many days." "How could you know of me, mother?" he asked. "I was told," she answered, "I would meet three illumined souls. I had met two and was looking for the third. Now I have found you."

Sri Ramakrishna's joy over the coming of the *Brahmani* was that of a lost child who has found its mother. There was no feeling of strangeness or shyness. He sat down beside her and poured out his inner perplexities and strivings with unquestioning confidence. The *Brahmani* was very learned. She knew by heart thousands of lines of sacred Sanskrit Scripture and she found in these an explanation for every state through which Sri Ramakrishna had passed or was passing. "You are not mad," she said to him in reassuring tones. "The fever that burns within you is the fever of God-intoxication. It is a holy madness, a madness born of divine ecstasy." Her words soothed his disquietude of spirit. He had come almost to doubt his own sanity, so unnatural even to himself was his behavior. She declared openly that she knew him to be a divine Manifestation and her claim was upheld by several *Pandits* who conferred with her at the Temple.

The *Brahmani* spent a few days at Dakshineswar talking hour after hour with Sri Ramakrishna, then he sent her to Devamandal's *Ghat* two miles away to find a lodging. The villagers there soon grew so devoted to her that they were eager to supply all her needs. She went daily to the Temple of Dakshineswar and sometimes Sri Ramakrishna came to her. He was like her own child and she gave him the love of a real mother; she guided all his *Sadhanas* and shared with him her Scriptural learning. She found him a ready pupil. It is told that he never needed to practise a *Sadhana* or spiritual exercise more than three days to attain its ultimate results. He himself said: "When I began a new practice, I prayed earnestly to Divine Mother to grant me its fruits and in three days at the most my prayer would be answered."

Mathura Babu and Hriday, the nephew, observed with open anxiety the close bond between the *Brahmani* and Sri Ramakrishna. They resented her dominating influence and the weight given to her words. They felt she played too large a part in the direction of his spiritual practices, that she sustained him in his madness, even accentuated it. Mathura Babu's displeasure was undisguised whenever he met the *Brahmani* at Dakshineswar. One day he asked her sharply: "*Brahmani*, where is your *Brahmana* (husband)?" She was just leaving the Temple of Divine Mother and she pointed to the image of the "Great God" within the Temple. "But He is motionless and without life," Mathura objected. "Why am I a *Bhairavi* (a religious renouncer)" she replied in spirited tones, "if I cannot infil a lifeless image with divine life and perceive the living Deity in it?" Afterwards Mathura learned to admire and revere her fine qualities; but Hriday never grew friendly towards her through all the eleven years she remained near Sri Ramakrishna and he became the immediate cause of her leaving.

I once asked Holy Mother what became of the *Brahmani* and I received this answer: "Once she went with Thakur (Sri Ramakrishna) to his village and I joined them. I did everything for her, cooked and served her in every way; but she and Hriday did not agree very well. One day they had a violent quarrel and after that she seemed altogether different. She was afraid to approach Thakur. If he spoke to her, she started and looked frightened. Always she was uneasy and restless. Not long after, she disappeared and no one knew where she had gone."

Others told me that towards the end the *Brahmani* grew overbearing and jealous of her rights and privileges. She seemed to feel that Sri Ramakrishna belonged to her and she coveted more and more authority over those who surrounded him. She regarded as an intrusion even the appearance at the Temple of the great monist teacher, Totapuri, and warned Sri Ramakrishna against his "dry and unfeeling" doctrine. As I heard of this gradual change after so much noble zeal and service there rose in my mind certain words spoken to me one day in Madras by the disciple Sasi: "The highest saint in heaven is not safe. The ego is always waiting to trap us. We can never afford to be off our guard."

Totapuri was one of the most powerful monistic teachers of his time. He was immovable in his disregard for bodily comforts and fleshly gratifications. For forty years he did not sleep under a roof. When food was not at hand he fasted for days with perfect unconcern. He refused to wear more than a loin cloth. Sometimes he cast that off even, but so wrapped about was he with exalted thought that no one was conscious of his nakedness. He never remained long anywhere, but wandered without weariness or flagging from holy place to holy place.

It was in the course of this unceasing pilgrimage that he came to Dakshineswar. As he entered the porch before the Divine Mother's Temple his eyes rested upon the modest figure of the young priest seated in meditation within the Sanctuary. The light on his face, the child-like humility of his bearing caught Totapuri's attention and interest at once. With unhesitating directness he walked to him and said: "Would you like to have me teach you?" "I will ask my Mother," was the young priest's reply. He entered the Temple and remained for some moments in prayer; then he came back with a bright smile on his face, saying: "Mother is willing, so I shall be glad to learn of you."

Without delay Totapuri began to instruct him in the lofty teachings of the *Adwaita* or monistic philosophy. His unknown pupil grasped the most abstruse of his doctrines with bewildering ease. He had taught him only a short while when he requested him to prepare to receive *Sannyas.* Sri

Ramakrishna had taken his first spiritual initiation some time before from a passing *Sannyasin* who came to the Temple, gave him the Holy Word or *Mantram,* then disappeared and was never heard from again.

Now he was to receive his final initiation from Totapuri. He consented without demur, but on one condition—that the ceremony be performed very quietly so that his aging earthly mother might be spared the shock of learning too suddenly of the new step, since it meant the severing of all earthly ties. Totapuri agreed to this and the new disciple made ready for the solemn rite.

The day arrived, the young priest with child-like obedience did everything as he was told. He went through the *Shraddha* or funeral rites to symbolize death to worldliness and rebirth in God. He sat by the sacred fire and cast into its flames all that typified earthly desire and habit, that out of the dimming embers of the human might rise a new glowing flame of the Divine. He let his head be shaven, the last crown lock was cut; his holy thread was removed; round his loins was tied the orange cloth, symbol of renunciation; and he was given the name of Ramakrishna. Gadadhar had ceased to be.

When the last rite was ended, Totapuri bade the newly-vowed *Sannyasin* sit in meditation and he himself took his seat near-by to shield him from intrusion. When, however, he saw that the young priest had gone beyond outward seeing and hearing, he went from the room, locking the door as a precaution against disturbance. The ceremony had taken place in the quiet hours of night. Morning dawned, the day passed and night came again, still no call from the room. Another day and night and a third, but not a sound. Then Totapuri, accustomed though he was to long periods of meditation, grew anxious and unlocked the door. There sat the figure just as he had left it, silent and motionless.

No doubt could there be regarding the total abstraction of the consciousness; scarcely a thread held it to the body. Yet Sri Ramakrishna was not unconscious. "*Samadhi* is never an unconscious state," the disciple Sasi once said to me. "When a man is in *Samadhi,* he is all-luminous, all-perfect. Even every particle of his body is fully conscious and illumined." Totapuri tested Sri Ramakrishna in every way, then he realized that he had reached the state of "seedless *Samadhi,*" the highest superconsciousness, that state of which Sri Ramakrishna himself said, if a man attained to it "he would live only twenty-one days and no food would ever again pass his lips. Connection with the physical was severed." A mighty mission, however, lay before the humble Temple priest and even *Nirvikalpa Samadhi* could not render it abortive. Quietly and cautiously Totapuri led him back to the outer world. As he touched it once more Totapuri exclaimed "What it has taken me forty years to gain, you have accomplished in a few days!"

Sri Ramakrishna had now entered upon the fourth stage of life, but he was never able to wear the orange cloth which marked it. Whenever he attempted to wind it about him, he would go into *Samadhi* and remain there. Nor was he able to tie even a white cloth, so the disciple Sasi told me. Some one had to do it for him. A knot means bondage and so complete was his realization of untrammelled freedom that he could take no part in binding or tying anything, not even a knot in a *Dhoti.* There were times when the few garments he wore dropped from him and he would be scarcely clothed at all, but he seemed so like a little child that no one gave it a thought.

From this moment sometimes Totapuri was the teacher, sometimes Ramakrishna. If Totapuri pointed a lesson, Ramakrishna by a few words carried the lesson deeper. Occasionally he even dared rebuke his elder. It is told that one day when Totapuri had prepared a sacred fire, a Temple servant took from it a burning brand to light his pipe. Totapuri, indignant at the desecration, drove him away. Sri Ramakrishna seeing this, exclaimed: "Where is your realization of oneness? You say all is Brahman, all is the Absolute, is not this man also a part of that Absolute?"

Through association with Sri Ramakrishna Totapuri gained a vision of God as Divine Mother, which tempered the rigidity of his monism and infused his nature with a new softness and radiance. This was the special gift Sri Ramakrishna was bringing to the world and he brought it among the first to Totapuri. So sweet to the tried and stern *Sannyasin* was this daily intercourse with the young priest of the Temple that he could not break it short. It had never been Totapuri's custom to remain in any one place more than three days that he might not be caught in the meshes of earthly attachment, but he lingered at the Temple of Dakshineswar for eleven months before he could persuade himself to set out once more on his unresting wanderings.

CONTACT WITH OTHER FORMS OF FAITH

The Temple of Dakshineswar stands out in impressive relief against the sky-line of the Ganges. Rani Rashmani was lavish in her votive offering. Twelve Shrines consecrated to the worship of the Third Person or Transforming Principle of the Vedic Trinity extend along the bank, divided from the river by a long narrow garden filled with fragrant flowering shrubs, a tidal rampart at its outer edge. At the centre of these twelve Shrines is an open pillared porch or *Mandapam,* from which one passes outward down a broad flight of steps to the main landing-ghat and inward to a vast court. In this, opposite the *Mandapam,* rises a massive Temple dedicated to the Divine Mother of the Universe. A smaller Temple adjoins it and the rest of the court is enclosed by a colonnade, like the twelve Shrines open only on the inner side.

In a front corner of the enclosure is a square room without windows but with three double doors —one opening on the colonnade, one on the Ganges and one towards the *Panchavati* or banyan grove. The room contains a wide bed, with a rude wooden couch beside it, several chests and a number of holy pictures. It was in this room that Sri Ramakrishna spent many years of his life. On this bed he slept, on this couch he sat to receive visitors or to meditate, before these sacred pictures he bowed his head at the evening hour, the hour of holy prayer. Previously he had occupied a lower room in the villa erected for the founder's family in the Temple compound.

Not far from the villa and close to the banyan grove is the Concert House where the various rites of the day are marked off in melody by the Temple musicians. Behind, at a little distance, lies the smaller pool, open to the sky. Shaded paths and a roadway curve in and out, leading in one direction to a great gate in the garden wall, in the other to the smaller *Ghat* or landing, where the women come for their daily bath in the Ganges. Wide slippery steps descend from the tidal wall to the water. To reach this *Ghat* the women must pass by the banyan tree with its platform where Sri Ramakrishna sat so long in meditation, and often when he was there some devout wife would stop and ask him to bless her with a child. It was these frequent interruptions which drove him to the greater seclusion of the Bel tree in the jungle beyond, where he and the cow were found.

Behind the main Temple enclosure lies the larger pool, green with the shadows of surrounding trees and bushes. Here one day Sri Ramakrishna saw a venerable Mohammedan sage standing, seemingly watching for him. Perceiving that he was a holy man, Sri Ramakrishna approached and greeted him with humble cordiality. This meeting marked the beginning of the second period of preparation. The first was over. Sri Ramakrishna had sounded the heights and depths of his own nature; now he must relate his individual experience to the spiritual experience of human-kind. There was, however, no calculation in his mind; no counting off of times or tasks. He moved forward naturally and spontaneously, in child-like obedience to the urge of his inner spirit.

He began questioning the Mohammedan about the tenets of his faith and the sage offered to instruct him in them. Sri Ramakrishna threw himself with ardor into his new study. He dressed like a Mohammedan, he ate like a Mohammedan, he lived like a Mohammedan, he studied Mohammedan Scriptures and followed Mohammedan religious practices. In order not to offend the conservative Brahmins associated with him in the Temple service, he remained and studied outside the Temple compound during this time; but the interval was so short, few had opportunity to discern what he was doing. Very soon he attained the same high point of vision he had reached through Vedic observance. His Mohammedan teacher was astounded by the swiftness of his attainment and paid him ready homage.

With the same zeal Sri Ramakrishna took up other religions and followed their customs and teaching. He assisted at worship in a Christian church. He read the Bible. He also sought a deeper understanding of the different forms of belief and different spiritual traditions among his own people. Always his study and practice brought him to the same lofty realization. He had proven beyond a doubt that "Many are the names of God and infinite the forms that lead us to know Him. Under whatsoever name, in whatsoever form you desire to call upon Him, in that very form and under that name you will see Him. As one and the same material water is called by different names by different peoples, one calling it water, another *eau,* a third *aqua* and another *pani,* so the one *Sat-Chit-Ananda,* Everlasting Intelligence and Bliss, is invoked by some as God, by some as Allah, by some as Jehovah, by some as Hari, by others as Brahman." These are Sri Ramakrishna's own words.

Such broad catholicity of feeling created an immediate relationship with the followers of every creed and sect. It made him one with every phase of thought, every expression of life, divine and human. The disciple Sasi told me: "When he talked of Sita, he would become Sita altogether, so that there would be absolutely no difference between him and Sita. If Vaishnava devotees came to him, at once he would become like Lord Gouranga. He would act, speak, look like Him—so much that the devotees would prostrate before him, saying: 'We see Lord Gouranga in you.'

"Once a Christian Quaker came to him, and as Ramakrishna talked of Christ, tears began to trickle down the man's face and he fell down clasping his feet and crying, 'I have found Christ in you.' In the same way when Mohammedans came, he would so completely identify himself with Mohammed that they would see their Prophet in Him. Yet behind all these different manifestations there was always the one Ramakrishna.

"The Vaishnavas were in the habit of holding *Bhajanam;* and regarding Sri Ramakrishna as a *Paramahamsa* (illumined soul) they once asked him to attend one of their meetings. In the hall where they met there was a high seat, which was regarded as Lord Gouranga's seat. It was the custom to begin their singing by invoking Lord Gouranga to come down and occupy his place, otherwise it would not be possible for them to praise the Lord properly, and it was actually believed that he did come down and sit on the seat. On that day when Ramakrishna was present, as soon as they began their invocation, he immediately got up, went and sat on the sacred seat. Some people thought it was all right, for he was known to be a very holy man; but others were indignant. Seeing, however, that he was in *Samadhi* and also perhaps being afraid of Hriday who was with him and who being a very stalwart man always acted as his body-guard, they did not dare disturb him.

"Among those who objected was a really great *Sadhu,* Bhagavan Das. He expressed his disapproval very boldly. The meeting nevertheless continued and Ramakrishna remained in Lord Gouranga's place. Some time after, hearing of the many things Bhagavan Das had said against him, Sri Ramakrishna expressed a wish to go to him. Mathura Babu procured a barge and they set out, but all the time Mathura Babu kept on saying: 'Why, Baba (father), do you want to go to that man? He must be a very wicked person to talk as he has. Why should we go there?' But Sri Ramakrishna answered: 'Let us go.' When they reached the place, instead of getting down himself, he sent Hriday to see whether the *Sadhu* cared to receive him. When Bhagavan Das heard that he had come, he ran to the barge and prostrated before him, crying: 'Oh forgive me, forgive me, I did not know who you were.' Ramakrishna at once comforted him and restored peace to his mind.

"Bhagavan Das was a really great *Sadhu* and he had the power now and then of entering into *Samadhi*. It seems that while he was in that state, it was revealed to him who Ramakrishna was and when he realized what a great mistake he had made, he was inconsolable. After that he went round telling every one that Ramakrishna had a right to take the seat, for he was a Divine Manifestation."

Sri Ramakrishna had abundant opportunity to come in contact with the adherents of different religious faiths. The lavish welcome given to every one at the Temple through Rani Rashmani's generosity drew an ever-growing number of pilgrims and devotees. At one period they seemed to come in groups. Invariably Sri Ramakrishna had a premonition of their coming and appealed to Mathura Babu to provide proper reception for them.

"At one time he expressed the desire to feed a large number of *Sadhus,* so a great quantity of hemp, *ghee* and other provisions was stored and for several months he was feeding thousands of *Sannyasins* who came to him from all directions," the disciple Sasi related to me. "At another time crowds of *Tantrikas* came. At still another time he wished to entertain *Vaishnavas* and he had thousands of *Tulasi* beads brought to him and for several months *Vaishnavas* came to him in great numbers.

"In those earlier years a desire would rise in his mind as if it came from the fountainhead of all desire and there was always the man to satisfy it in Mathura Babu. He looked upon Ramakrishna as Divinity itself. One day when Mathura was in the Temple garden, he saw a figure on the river wall, as if the Divine Mother had come out of Her Temple and was walking along the rampart. Involuntarily he fell down and prostrated before Her. Then he found that it was really Ramakrishna in whom he had seen the Mother. From that moment he never wanted to leave his side and he was ready to do anything for him.

"When Sri Gurumaharaj (Ramakrishna) expressed a wish to go to Benares Mathura Babu engaged a private coach with the understanding that it was to be detached from the train whenever they chose. Every morning they were put on a side track. Then Gurumaharaj would have his bath and his breakfast, after which another train would pick them up and carry them on. Whenever he would see a starving, half-clad man or woman he would insist on the person being well-fed and clothed before he would continue his journey.

"At one place the people were all so poor and wretched that some had not even a loin cloth. Gurumaharaj got down from the train and said: 'I shall not stir from here until all these people have received proper cloths and been generously fed for fifteen days.' At once Mathura ordered bales of cloths to be brought from Calcutta, a large number of cooks were hired and thousands of poor people were fed while Gurumaharaj looked on, enjoying the sight."

He felt little real interest in journeys or pilgrimages, however. On his return from Benares his comment was: "The grass is just as green at Dakshineswar as it was at Benares." He was content to remain in quiet obscurity, spending his time in communing with his Divine Mother and in transmitting Her message to those who sought it. He never made claim to the teaching he gave. His attitude was voiced in this prayer which was constantly on his lips:—

"Mother, I am *Yantra* (the machine), Thou art *Yantri* (one who works the machine); I am the room, Thou art the tenant; I am the sheath, Thou art the sword; I am the chariot, Thou art the charioteer. I do just as Thou makest me do; I speak as Thou makest me speak; I behave as Thou makest me behave. Not I, not I, but Thou."

The pilgrimage with Mathura Babu included Allahabad and Vrindavan and they talked of going to Gaya, but Sri Ramakrishna felt the call of the Temple and its life of quiet communion, so they turned back. The quietude he sought, however, was not to last. As the days passed it was broken more and more frequently. The rumor had gone abroad that a great *Paramahamsa* had appeared at the Temple of Dakshineswar and people came in multiplying numbers to see him. Some came out of curiosity, others to question and learn, still others to scoff and disconcert; but after a few moments in his presence even the most skeptical was forced to admit that behind the veil of simplicity and child-like humility which enveloped him, a Great Light was shining. The humility and simplicity were a proof of the light.

"A *Paramahamsa* is like a little child," the disciple Saśi declared. "While, however, a little child through its ignorance, sees everything as living, the *Paramahamsa* sees everything as living through his wisdom. This is the difference. So a *Paramahamsa* is called a child and not a child, mad and not mad. How can he be mad when he is the repository of all wisdom? A *Paramahamsa*, being infinitely wise sees God everywhere, and for this reason he never wants for anything.

"Suppose you have a millionaire for your best friend, will he let you have any want? If he sees you with a torn cloth, will he not give you a new one? If he finds you have not eaten, will he not at once order food to be brought? In the same way, when a man has made friends with God, his want of wisdom, his want of bliss, his want of life, he will get rid of at once. How can he want for life, when all lives come out of God? How can he want for bliss when God is made up of pure bliss? How can he want for wisdom when God is the source of all wisdom? Therefore since God is the friend of the *Paramahamsa*, He will not let him lack for anything. This is why God says: 'Between Me and My devotee there is no difference: My wisdom is his wisdom, My life is his life, My bliss is his bliss.' "

AT THE TEMPLE

Prior to his pilgrimage, Sri Ramakrishna spent several months in his native village. He had begun to show the strain of his intensive spiritual practice and Mathura Babu and others thought a change to the quieter atmosphere of Kamarpukur might rest and refresh him. The *Brahmani* and Hriday accompanied him and it was during this visit that the *Brahmani* disappeared. Sri Ramakrishna, however, saw her the following year at Benares and not long after she passed away.

There were other later journeys to the village and on one of these an incident occurred which disclosed an unsuspected aspect of Sri Ramakrishna's nature. The disciple Sasi told me of it thus:—

"Although Sri Gurumaharaj seemed so fragile, he manifested at times the strength of a giant. Once with another he was crossing the wide plain going to his native village. Just in the middle there came the cry, 'Decoits are coming.' In those parts these robbers are very terrible and will kill a man for a quarter Anna. The palanquin bearers without a word dropped their burden and ran away, leaving Gurumaharaj alone with his companion who was at a loss to know what to do. Gurumaharaj, apparently not in the least anxious, stood silent until the decoits had almost overtaken them, then he gave such a blood-curdling yell that they fled in terror. It seemed to fill all space and not to come from any human throat. As he saw the robbers run away he smiled. Then he set out and walked to his village with such long, rapid strides that his companion, although a much more robust man, scarcely could keep pace with him."

It was no longer Chandra Devi, the mother, who drew him to Kamarpukur. She had come to live at the Temple. With all his abstraction from outer things, Sri Ramakrishna had never faltered in his tender loyalty to her; and as he had seen her aging, he had brought her near that he might give her more vigilant care. It was chiefly mindfulness of her which led him to cut short his pilgrimage to the north. For a moment he had felt a desire to linger at Vrindavan. He had met there a very saintly woman, by name Ganga-Ma, who was regarded with great reverence because of her exceptional spiritual attainment. She was quite old, but she lived alone in a little hut, devoting her time to meditation and to helping by holy words those who came to her for counsel or cheer. She was very eager to have Sri Ramakrishna remain at Vrindavan; but as he looked at her furrowed face, thoughts of an aging, waiting mother-heart at Dakshineswar called him back and he insisted on returning to the Temple beside the Ganges.

While all this was taking place Saradamani, the young wife, was living quietly at Jayramvati with her parents. She had passed from childhood to girlhood and from girlhood to womanhood in her village home, with scarcely a sign from her husband. Once only had she had the blessing of being near him for a time. When he had paid the long visit to Kamarpukur in 1867, he had sent for her and had taught her as he had done at the time of the marriage. Then she was a little girl, now she was fourteen years old—almost a woman. Her husband's gentle holiness and unassuming wisdom had called forth in her a deep and reverent love and she harbored in her soul a mute longing to be near him and serve him.

She waited for five more years, then an unexpected opportunity presented itself. Certain relatives were going on pilgrimage to Calcutta and she asked to go with them. Her father also accompanied her and they set out all together, meaning to travel the seventy-five or eighty miles on foot. Their scant resources made it impossible to hire a palanquin and bearers. The fatigues of the journey proved too great for Saradamani and she fell ill on the way. When at last she reached Dakshineswar she was wan and weak. Sri Ramakrishna manifested the deepest concern and gave her the tenderest care, but her coming roused grave perplexity in his mind. In all women he saw Divine Mother: how could he regard one of them as a wife? Sarada's answer to this question quieted his troubled thought. "I only ask to serve and learn," she said. He consented that she remain and when she had grown strong enough, he sent her to the Concert House to care for his mother.

"I was about eighteen when I first came to Dakshineswar," she herself told me while I was with her in Calcutta. "I stayed there one year at that time, then returned for awhile to my village. In all I lived at the Temple fifteen or sixteen years. When I first went there, Thakur's mother was still living and he would come two or three times a day to sit with her, while I was busy with my household duties. After she passed away I lived at the Concert House alone. The music was played upstairs and I had the little room downstairs with the verandah, which was carefully screened. Only through one little opening could I see the outside world and I would watch there all day and night just to catch one glimpse of Thakur, but when he passed he would draw his cloth across his face. Thus days went by without my seeing him. In course of time, however, Gopal-ma, Yogin-ma and other lady devotees came and I was less alone.

"Every morning I used to get up at three o'clock and go for my bath in the Ganges. Once when I was going down the steps to the bathing-ghat, I saw something dark in the water. I called to a woman who was following me that there was something there. She replied: 'Oh, it is nothing but one of the big pots for boiling rice which they have thrown away.' As it moved up and down in the water, I, too, thought it might be that; but just before I reached it, it gave a plunge and I saw that it was a big crocodile. If I had gone down one more step, it would have caught me.

"After my bath I would return to my little room in the Concert House and not leave it again all day. The sun never came there so I could not dry my hair properly. The *Purdah* curtain round the verandah was just above the height of a man's head. All of Thakur's disciples used to come with provisions and I had to cook for them, so round the edge of the little room there were cooking vessels, bags of rice, *dal,* etc. I slept in the small space in the middle.

"Some time later I fell ill and one of the *Bhaktas* (devotees) of Thakur said I must move to another house, so he gave two large trunks of trees, costing five hundred Rupees, to build one. These were brought up the Ganges and I told Hriday that he must tie them to the shore, otherwise the tide would come up and float them off. But Hriday tied only the outer one, and in the night the tide rose and floated the other one away and they had much difficulty in recovering it. In the morning Hriday began to scold me saying: 'It is your lack of faith that caused all this trouble.' But Thakur said: 'Why are you scolding her? It is because you neglected to tie the log that it has got away.' The logs were sawed up and a little house built for me in the village near the Temple. There I lived with Lakididi and a maid-servant to care for me.

"One day Thakur said: 'All the Brahmins come to the Temple, take the *Prasad* (blessed food), tie it in their cloth and carry it home. I, too, shall do like them.' So he took the *Prasad*, tied it in his cloth, threw it over his shoulder and walked to my house in the village. 'Here is *Prasad* for you, give me some of the food you have prepared for yourselves,' he said. 'But we have cooked only rice for us and you cannot eat rice. You would better take the *Prasad*,' I replied. 'No, no,' he insisted, 'all the other Brahmins take the food the ladies of the house have prepared and give the *Prasad* to them. I must do the same.' So he ate our food and then he said he wanted to spend the night there. 'But there is no bedstead. It will not be possible for you,' Hriday objected. 'How do the ladies sleep?' Sri Ramakrishna asked. 'On the floor.' 'Then prepare me a bed like them,' he said.

"A mat was put down for him and he and Hriday slept in one corner of the room, and Lakididi, the maid-servant and I in the other. On the following morning when he was returning early to the Temple, he met one of his *Bhaktas*, who asked him where he had been so early. 'I am coming from my house,' he said, and the *Bhakta* laughed, thinking he was merely making fun.

"Hriday's wife who was stopping in the village near the Temple chanced to be ill at one time. She had a maid-servant with her, but I also went to nurse her, while Hriday remained with Thakur. It was the rainy season and he was not well. As Hriday had all the worship in the Temple besides serving and cooking for Thakur, I was anxious lest Thakur would not receive proper care; so my thought was constantly with him and I found it very hard to stay with Hriday's wife. Suddenly there appeared at Hriday's house a Brahmin lady who said: 'Why should you stay here? Your heart is all the time at the Temple. This servant can do what is needful here. Come back to Thakur.' So she took me back to the Temple and together we would nurse Thakur at night.

"I was always so shy when I came to him that I drew my veil down to my chin. He would ask me why I veiled myself and tell me to lift it. But I could not draw it up beyond my nose. One night, however, I remember he talked the whole night of the Lord and I became, as it were, mad. When dawn broke I found myself standing before him with my veil thrown entirely back from my face and lost in what he was saying. The daylight suddenly recalled me to myself. I drew my veil quickly and ran to the Concert House.

"Once I asked Thakur with what name I should make *Japam*. He looked up at me so searchingly that I was frightened and blushed. He replied: 'Take any name you like. Only believe that all power lies in the name you choose and it will surely save you.'

"I spent much time in my village also; but whenever Mathura Babu would say to Thakur: 'Why do you not have Mother come and cook for you?' he would send for me and I would go to the Temple for a time. During his last illness I asked to come and be near him and he allowed me to do so. Then when I would bring his noonday meal, I would sit by him for an hour, fanning and serving him."

These, Saradamani Devi's own words, give glimpses of her life at the Temple. Her days passed in loving, self-forgetting service, but some looked with questioning eyes on her presence there. "There was a *Bhakta* (devotee) by the name of Yogin who spent much time with Gurumaharaj. One day the maid servant, Brinda, said to him: 'Your *Paramahamsa* is a fraud. He pretends to be very pious all the day, but when night comes and every one is sleeping, he slips away and spends his time with his wife.' This implanted a doubt in Yogin's mind and he determined to remain for a night at Dakshineswar and see for himself what happened. Just at midnight he saw Gurumaharaj's door open, while in the bright moonlight he could see Holy Mother sitting in meditation on the upper verandah of the Concert House. Gurumaharaj walked toward it, passed quickly by and went on down to the *Panchavati* to meditate.

"Overpowered by a sense of the unworthy suspicion of which he had been guilty, Yogin followed the Master and threw himself down at his feet, begging his pardon. Gurumaharaj smilingly reassured him, then added: 'It would do no good to go to Mother. She is not in this world. Her soul has gone far above it. Did you not see her as you passed?'" This incident was related to me by a direct disciple of the Master. It shows how unfailingly tolerant and forgiving was Sri Ramakrishna's habit.

Sri Ramakrishna's mother lived to be over one hundred and three. She came to live at the Temple in 1863; it was not until 1872 that the young wife, her daughter-in-law, was brought to serve her. Then her mental power was fast waning, but the ardor of her spiritual devotion for the Lord had not weakened. She was as faithful in her religious habit as she had been throughout her younger days. In Bengal it is the custom to blow the conch shell at the close of the worship and in village and town one catches the melodious sound from this house, then from that, as the hour of prayer comes to an end. The meal is not eaten until it has been offered and this offering takes place as a part of the worship.

Chandra would never eat before the worship. There was a factory not far from the Temple and when the noon whistle blew loudly she took it for the conch shell of heaven and would say:

"Now they have finished worship in heaven. I will eat." But on Sunday there was no whistle and she refused to take food, saying: "It is not time. They have not finished worship in heaven." That she might not fast, they made an imitation factory whistle at the Temple, but when Sunday arrived and it sounded, Chandra Devi exclaimed: "Something must be wrong in heaven to-day, the conch shell is so weak," and she refused her food.

The mother passed away in 1876. Sri Ramakrishna's grief was poignant. He came seldom to the Concert House and when Saradamani Devi was at the Temple she was much alone; but she filled her moments of aloneness with devout spiritual practice and meditation and in her heart she was content and peaceful.

KESHAB CHANDRA SEN

Sri Ramakrishna did not live at the Temple in pompous waiting for the world to come and pay him homage. He coveted obscurity. Publicity and self-assertion were alien to his nature. He cared little to be seen and known of men, but he was always eager to give honor to others. When he heard that Devendra Nath Tagore, the poet's father, with all his wealth and many worldly claims still found ample leisure and occasion to think on God, he asked to be taken to see him. After hearing his conception of Deity and talking with him on various grave subjects, he remarked with humble satisfaction that Devendra Nath's spiritual experience coincided with his own.

One purpose of his pilgrimage to Benares was to visit a noted sage. Mathura Babu provided him with suitable offerings and he carried them to the *Sadhu* in utmost humility, prostrating before him like the least of pilgrims. At another time he heard of a holy Brahmin living in a distant quarter of Calcutta. Again he made request to go. Mathura Babu took him and Sri Ramakrishna laughed heartily over the incongruity of Mathura's huge stately carriage standing in front of the Brahmin's tiny hut. It was a spontaneous impulse with him to seek out holiness and superior merit.

Thus it was that when word was brought to the Temple that the great leader of the Nabobidhan

Brahmo Samaj, Keshab Chandra Sen, was in a garden adjoining the Temple compound, Sri Ramakrishna at once expressed the desire to go and meet him. The garden was a familiar spot to Sri Ramakrishna. Its owner was a devoted friend and frequently Sri Ramakrishna walked there in the cool hours of the day when the air was permeated with the sweet odors of flowers and aromatic shrubs. It was in one of its shaded paths also that he had had a remarkable vision of Jesus, a vision which had awakened in him a new sense of closeness to the Christian teaching and the Christ Ideal.

He found Keshab Chandra Sen surrounded by a number of his disciples. The contrast between the obscure Temple priest and the noted Brahmo leader was striking—the priest in simplest dress, with unassuming manner; the Brahmo leader in finest linen, with majestic bearing; one distinctively an Easterner, embodying the tradition and glory of Vedic India; the other wearing on his person, in his manner and his trend of thought the obvious stamp of Western influence. They seemed to stand at opposite poles, the prophet of the old and the prophet of the new.

The Brahmo Samaj was essentially modern in its character. It represented a reaction and protest against ceremonial, caste, social custom and all that savored of ancient conservatism. There were moderates among them, it is true, who desired only to prune and graft; but there were also extremists who wished to cut to the very root. Both have had in some degree a salutary effect on Indian society in removing or modifying certain social and religious distortions and traditional excesses, just as the Unitarians have contributed their share towards the general religious readjustment of the Occident. The Brahmo movement corresponds in many ways to the Unitarian reaction against orthodoxy.

In contrast to Keshab Chandra Sen, Sri Ramakrishna lacked the background of a definite organization. He had founded nothing. His following was in the making. His mission was undefined and unexpressed. He appeared even unaware of it. His method, too, was totally different from that of the Brahmo reformer. Keshab discarded, Sri Ramakrishna readjusted and utilized. He gathered up and made space for all phases of belief, for every custom and Scriptural injunction, finding the natural place of each in the universal gradation of human thought. He related every aspect of the evolving finite to infinitude. Yet all the while he remained a rigid and conservative observer of religious rites, of caste, of tradition, of Vedic idealism as a whole.

"In the years before Keshab came to him, his life was peculiar. He could then only associate with orthodox Brahmins. But after Keshab came he began to teach and associate with all sorts of people. It was really through Keshab that he became known to the world, especially to the young men of the day. It cannot be said that any of Ramakrishna's disciples came to him directly through Keshab Chandra Sen; but Keshab's devotion to him undoubtedly had much influence in leading them to go to him." This was said to me by the disciple Sasi.

It was not that contact with the founder of the New Dispensation, as Keshab's Samaj was called, altered Sri Ramakrishna's point of view. Ultimate vision was already his. But it marked the beginning of a new era in his outer life. I will give the picture of the meeting as it was given to me by the disciple Sasi. I use his words whenever it is possible, because they have the value of direct testimony, coming through him from Sri Ramakrishna himself.

"The first time Gurumaharaj went to Keshab Sen, before Keshab knew who he was, Keshab merely nodded his head in English fashion, but Gurumaharaj prostrated at full length before him —which so abashed Keshab that when Gurumaharaj left, he could not help but bow a little lower. Later when Keshab came to know who he was he would prostrate reverently at his feet.

"He used to urge Ramakrishna to come to his Brahmo Samaj and once Ramakrishna went. When Keshab saw him enter he came down from his high seat and wanted Gurumaharaj to take his place there. But Gurumaharaj said: 'No, No; go on with your exercises as you always have them.' He had no desire to enter into rivalry with Keshab or usurp his high place. He used to pray: 'Let all name and fame belong to Keshab, O Mother! Grant only that I may have true devotion for Thy Holy Feet.'

"Once he was invited to attend a theatrical performance given by Keshab's Samaj. One of the members of the Brahmo Samaj in talking with him said: 'Keshab is such a great lover of God, he must be an incarnation of Lord Gouranga and Mazumdar is always his companion, so he must be an incarnation of Nityananda. Now who are you?' Gurumaharaj clasped his hands, bowed his head and replied: 'I am their servant.' When Keshab heard of this conversation, he turned to the man and said: 'You fool! How could you talk in such a senseless way?'

"Sri Gurumaharaj found genuine delight in Keshab Chandra Sen's companionship. When he heard that Keshab was mortally ill, he exclaimed: 'Mother, if you take Keshab, with whom will I talk of God?' Gurumaharaj loved Keshab Sen very much. He used to say that he enjoyed talking with no one so much as with Keshab, because he asked so many high questions. When Gurumaharaj described the different steps in the spiritual life, Keshab would always ask 'And after that what comes?' 'And again after that?'

"One day Gurumaharaj was explaining to him the different stages of *Bhakti* (devotion). Keshab asked eagerly: 'And then what comes?' 'Keshab, if I tell you,' Gurumaharaj replied, 'You will have to give up your teaching; all idea of teacher and student will disappear. Are you ready for that?' 'No,' Keshab replied, 'I do not wish to go so far.' At that time he was the *Guru* of thousands, who looked to him for guidance, and he felt it his duty to help humanity. Sri Gurumaharaj used to declare that Keshab was an eternal worker of God and would have to come again and again to help mankind.

"Keshab on his side often said: 'If any one wants to know what purity is, what true religion is, he will have to go to Dakshineswar and sit at the feet of Sri Ramakrishna Paramahamsa. He is the embodiment of the New Dispensation which I am preaching. I preach it, but he is living it.' It was these reiterated words of Keshab which led many to go to see Sri Ramakrishna. They said: 'If Keshab Sen, who disbelieves so strongly in image-worship, can speak thus of a Brahmin priest, a Temple worshipper, he must be a true *Paramahamsa.*' "

These two God-chosen figures were frequently together. There is record of a wonderful day on the Ganges when Keshab came to the Temple in a steamer and carried Sri Ramakrishna off for an outing on the river. Sri Ramakrishna sang holy songs and talked hour after hour of God, personal and impersonal, formful and formless; of the create and uncreate; of soul and body; of the bliss of communion with the Blissful Mother of the universe. His words flowed from his lips in joyous stream, with now and then a holy pause as, swept by some exalted thought, he passed from outer consciousness into super-conscious silence.

A numerous group of gentlemen, guests of Keshab Chandra Sen, sat round him in the deck cabin of the steamer, all of them held spellbound by the subtle and lofty beauty of his teaching. The beauties of sky and shore and river were forgotten, time and place faded away, nothing remained but this modest Brahmin who seemed a giant in his wisdom, a little child in the simplicity of his manner and mode of expression.

It was in 1875 that the first meeting took place. Keshab Chandra Sen passed away in 1884. The intervening years were full of many happy associations. When Sri Ramakrishna learned that the end was near, he went to Keshab's home to see him. Although for some time Keshab had been confined to his own apartment, he insisted on coming to the drawing-room to greet Sri Ramakrishna. He requested him to take his seat on a raised couch while he himself sat down on the floor before him, but Sri Ramakrishna slipped to the floor beside Keshab and lifting Keshab's wasted hand, he weighed it tenderly in his own, grieving over its lightness.

He talked with him for a long time, speaking exalting words and words of comfort. "The Bussora rose is of a superior variety," he said. "The gardener clears away the soil from around the roots that the night dew may reach them. The dew brings new strength and freshness to the plant. So the Divine Gardener knows how to deal with you, Keshab. He is digging round about you to the very roots that the dew of His inspiration shall fall on you more abundantly and make you mightier than ever." Many more words he spoke, but a violent fit of coughing forced Keshab to cut the conversation short. He prostrated before Sri Ramakrishna in parting salutation and slowly left the room, holding to the wall as he walked.

There are other Brahmo organizations. The Adi Brahmo Samaj, founded by Ram Mohan Roy and Devendra Nath Tagore, is the parent Samaj. It is to this that the poet, Ravindra Nath Tagore, and all his family belong. It is much less radical in its methods and has instituted fewer changes. It retains more of the Vedic traditions than the Nabobidhan Brahmo Samaj or "New Dispensation" of Keshab Chandra Sen, which bears the deepest tinge of Western influence. Then there is the Sadharan Brahmo Samaj composed of seceding members of Keshab's Samaj.

Sri Ramakrishna counted warm friends in all the societies. Bijoy Krishna Goswami, the leader of the Sadharan Samaj, was a fervent admirer of Sri Ramakrishna. He visited him at the Temple and sought his counsel. Once when Sri Ramakrishna was present at a religious meeting where Bijoy was to conduct the Service, Bijoy came humbly to him and said: "Please give me your blessing. Without your blessing I cannot begin." "Who am I to bless?" Sri Ramakrishna replied. "Ask the blessing of the Lord. Where there is true humility, there is no fear." Bijoy reiterated his request and at last Sri Ramakrishna acceded, saying: "Go now and begin, but keep your mind fixed on God."

When the Service was over, Bijoy asked "How can one attain the vision of Divine Mother?" Sri Ramakrishna's answer was: "Pray and cry aloud in earnest and sincere longing. When the heart is purified, the vision will be seen as the sun's reflection is seen in clear water. Upon the mirror of the purified heart of the devotee the reflection of the Divine Mother will shine forth; but the mirror must be cleansed and polished. If there is one speck of dust, the reflection will not be perfect."

Many more words he spoke while a large gathering listened reverently. "Sri Ramakrishna never preached," the disciple Sasi told me. "If he went anywhere it was to be among good men and be blessed by their holy association. That was his idea. But when he was there Divine Mother would rise up in him and he would begin to talk. It mattered not whether there were few listeners or many."

All branches of the Brahmo Samaj adopted congregational worship, which is foreign to the Indian manner of approaching Deity. According to the Indian conception, true worship means communion and Divine communion calls for aloneness with God. The Temple is the sanctifying centre of the community, the place where the presence of Deity is felt in greater fullness. It is the specific home of the universal Mother and Father, where the children come, not in delegations, but singly, to lay down their burdens and share their joys. Congregational worship is peculiarly Western. It possesses undoubtedly certain beneficent qualities. It inspires and stimulates; but also it affords multiple opportunities for distracting and scattering the mind. That Sri Ramakrishna recognized this is shown by this incident related to me by a disciple.

"Sri Ramakrishna once attended a religious meeting at which many hundreds of people were present. When the meeting was over, the leader came down and asked him what he thought of the meditation and the earnestness of his congregation. 'At evening time,' Gurumaharaj replied, 'the monkeys are very sedate and quiet, but all the time they are thinking: 'There is a fine cucumber in a certain old lady's garden; to-morrow I will go and steal it.' Or: 'To-day I saw a fine gourd hanging by the wayside, in the morning I will get it.' All these people are like that. They look very grave and pious but they are all the time thinking how they can buy and sell and make more money.' "

There was no malice in Sri Ramakrishna's words. They were spoken with a smile, but they carried a lesson. He had no quarrel with any form of religious observance, but he demanded sincerity behind it and tolerance as its basis. "Go on," he once said to a gathering of Brahmos, "what you are doing is good, but do not run away with the idea that yours is the only way."

THE FIRST DISCIPLES

Around Keshab Chandra Sen had gathered a group of young men who were not accredited members of the Nabobidhan Brahmo Samaj, but who looked to it for inspiration and spiritual stimulus. They were ardent admirers of Keshab, his methods and his ideals. They had thrown off the trammels of orthodoxy, had broken caste, had rebelled against the traditions of their ancient faith and had yielded to the lure of Western science and Western rationalism. Their minds seemed to offer soil poorly adapted for a message such as Sri Ramakrishna had to give, yet it was here that Keshab's words about the *Paramahamsa* of Dakshineswar took deepest root. They said among themselves: "If Keshab Chandra Sen, whom we honor so much, shows such great reverence for this *Paramahamsa,* there must be something extraordinary in him."

The most dominant figure in this group was Narendra Nath Dutt, "Naren" as he was called familiarly. In later years his brother disciples nearly always spoke of him as "Swamiji." "He was a devoted follower of Keshab Sen," so the disciple Sasi told me. "Keshab did not seem to regard him as anything more than the other boys around him, but Naren had a beautiful voice, so he was asked to sing in the choir of the Brahmo Samaj. In those days we were all arch skeptics.

We prided ourselves on being purely rationalistic and did not believe in God or religion. Naren was an absolute disbeliever. He said, 'This creation is self-existent, automatic; what need therefore of a God?'

"Whenever he heard of a great devotee he would at once go to him and ask: 'Sir, do you believe in God?' 'Yes,' the sage would reply. 'Have you seen Him?' 'Oh, no! I have not seen Him!' 'Then what do you meditate upon?' 'Oh, we are told that He is here in the heart. I think of Him there.' 'My dear sir,' Naren would say, 'this is all your imagination. You are a sane man. You ought to be more intelligent.' So he went from one to another advising each not to be duped by his imagination. If there was a *Bhajana* party, he would ridicule them, saying: 'Look at these mad fellows singing the praises of a God of whose existence they know nothing.' In this way he became a terror to every one.

"One day when he had been talking to a relative, the man said: 'You are a hopeless disbeliever, but come with me to Dakshineswar; there is a *Paramahamsa* there who can, I believe, destroy your doubts.' So Naren went. When he saw Gurumaharaj he thought, 'What sort of mad man is this?' But Gurumaharaj received him kindly, asked him to sit down and then inquired whether he knew how to sing. Ramakrishna had a way of searching out a man's special talents. Naren sang two or three of the Brahmo hymns. Then Gurumaharaj inquired who he was and his relative described him as a thorough disbeliever. Gurumaharaj said it was not good to doubt and Naren asked: 'Have you seen God?' 'Oh, yes,' Gurumaharaj at once replied. 'Can you make me see Him now?' 'Yes, I can,' Gurumaharaj answered, 'But it is better to come alone. Can you come tomorrow?' Naren was still not sure he was not mad, but Naren was never a coward, so he said: 'Yes, I will come.'

"Naren never told a lie in his life, so the next day, although he had some misgivings, he returned to the Temple. Gurumaharaj was sitting on the bedstead talking apparently to some one although there was no one in the room. Naren thought 'He must surely be mad to sit here and talk when there is no one to listen,' so he sat down a little away from him. But Gurumaharaj said, 'Come and sit here,' pointing to the foot of the couch beside him. Naren, being always fearless, went, ready to defend himself.

"When he had sat down, Gurumaharaj leaned over and touched his heart through the front of his shirt which was unbuttoned. Naren told me afterwards: 'The walls of the room began to recede and disappear. Then the river and all Calcutta vanished. The floor of the room seemed to sink down into the earth, until at last I seemed to be in a vast vacuum in which there was nothing but this Brahmin standing before me.' This is how he told it but Gurumaharaj in speaking of it afterwards said that as he felt all this happening he exclaimed: 'What are you doing? I have my mother, my brothers to look after.' But Naren did not remember this.

"Gurumaharaj in telling the story of Naren's first coming, said, 'When I saw this boy enter the room I thought, can such a boy come out of Calcutta where everyone is mad after money and pleasure—where everything is *Rajasika* (feverishly active)? I could see that his mind was three-fourths turned inward and only with the other fourth was he doing all these outer things. One corner of his shawl was dragging on the ground, his hair was a little dishevelled, as if he was careless about such things.'

"Later, when I asked Sri Ramakrishna whether there was a God, he told me to go to the boy Narendra and ask him. I went and asked him. Then Naren told me this story and he added that for fifteen or twenty days after this he seemed to see God everywhere. Everything seemed to be living, the ground, the wall, everywhere was life. So he came to know that this Brahmin was no ordinary *Paramahamsa*."

How the simple Brahmin of the Temple felt towards Naren is made plain by this incident recounted to me by Yogin-ma, a devout householder disciple of the Master:—

"Once Naren had not come to the Temple for some time and Thakur (Ramakrishna) growing impatient to see him, came to Balaram's house and sent for him. Naren came at his free hour. When it was nearly time for him to return to college, Thakur came to the ladies' quarters and called me. 'Naren must go back to college, can you not give him something to eat?' he asked. Then he added, (and he had such a winning way, no one could resist him) 'You have little boys who go to school, you must have made some simple curries for them. Can you not spare some for Naren? He is such a good boy.' I took some rice and a few curries and carried them to Naren. When he had eaten, Thakur told me to pour water over his hands, repeating: 'He is such a good boy.' Then Naren went back to his college but he came again later in the day." This is the first time Yogin-ma saw Naren.

"Narendra was about nineteen when he came to Gurumaharaj," the disciple Sasi told me, "but despite his youth he was carrying a heavy burden. His father, a lawyer, had died the previous year, leaving the financial affairs of the family very much involved. They had a large and imposing home but no money, and Naren had great trouble in providing for the immediate necessities of his household. Often he had to go without a meal. Once he had had no food for two days. He came that evening to the house of a friend where Gurumaharaj had also come. Gurumaharaj was eating, with Latu by his side. As he ate, Latu mixed some curry with rice, walked across and laughingly threw it into Naren's mouth. Naren told me that at once he felt all full, as if he had eaten a hearty meal. Then he realized the meaning of Christ's answer to the devil: 'Man does not live by bread alone, but by every word that proceedeth out of the mouth of God.' He knew that Gurumaharaj was acting through Latu.

"The financial difficulties of the family grew more and more serious. A law-suit added to them. No money was available to engage legal advice. Finally, there came a day when no one else would lend him money and there was no food in the house. Not knowing what to do, Naren went to Dakshineswar. Gurumaharaj saw that his mind was much troubled and when he heard the cause he said: 'Go to the Mother's Temple and ask Her to help you.' Narendra went, prayed and came back. 'What did you pray for?' Gurumaharaj asked. 'I prayed for more *Bhakti* (devotion) for the Mother's Holy Feet. I could not ask for money.' 'Go and try again,' Gurumaharaj said. On his return again he asked: 'What did you pray for?' 'I prayed that I might have more *Vairagyam* (renunciation) and more *Bhakti* (devotion),' was his answer. 'You have done well, my boy.' Gurumaharaj then said: 'From henceforth your family will never lack for the necessities of life.' And since that time, although they have never been rich, the family has always had enough.

"From the outset Gurumaharaj's love for Naren was unbounded. When Naren did not come to the Temple for a time, Gurumaharaj would grow so restless that he would weep even. Once when I was with him, he kept running first to the Ganges side, then to the road side, to see whether Naren was coming. At last he told me to bring a carriage. I ran two miles off to get one and together we drove to Naren's house. We found him in his dingy room on the ground floor. 'Why have you come?' he asked with evident annoyance on seeing Gurumaharaj. 'What will my family think when they see a *Sadhu* coming to see me like this?' In reality, however, he was annoyed that Gurumaharaj should have paid him so much honor.

"At the time when Naren went to see Pahauri Baba and remained away for three weeks, Gurumaharaj wept bitterly, crying: 'I have lost the crown-jewel from my head.' Naren's unselfishness and loving-kindness had no limit. Even as a child he possessed such a quick, sympathetic heart that if he saw a beggar in the street, he would run upstairs, snatch one of his mother's best *Saris* and throw it from the window. There was no one more tolerant in the matter of mistakes. If any one committed a blunder he would say: 'That is very good. How could we learn, if we did not commit blunders?' He never condemned the man.

"Once when we were returning from Dakshineswar, Naren insisted on taking me home with him. His mother had saved his supper for him, but without letting me know it, he gave this to me and went without food himself. When bed-time came, he put me on his cot under the mosquito curtain. I was very tired and fell asleep at once. In the morning when I woke, I found that Naren had spent the night on the bare floor at the other side of his room.

"He was very indifferent to his surroundings. In his own house he lived in a dark damp room on the ground floor. Books lay about everywhere. On the fire was always a pot of tea. Here he would sit and read, lost in his thoughts. When he grew tired or hungry he would drink a tumbler of the tea boiling hot and then go on with his study.

"While he was still attending college he used to study all day and spend the night in meditation. This constant use of the brain brought on a severe pain in his head which kept him rolling on his bed for several days. Hearing of it Gurumaharaj came to the house of a devotee near by and sent for him. 'But he cannot get up from his bed,' some one explained. 'Just tell him, he will come,' Gurumaharaj replied. Naren came and as he sat down by Gurumaharaj, the latter ran his hand lovingly through his hair saying: 'Why, my boy, what is the matter? You have a headache have you?' Naren said that at once all the pain left him.

"Once a drama by Keshab was to be performed and to Naren was assigned the part of a *Sannyasin* (monk). Gurumaharaj expressed great satisfaction when he heard of it and insisted on being taken to see the performance. Naren acquitted himself most creditably of his task and after the play was over Gurumaharaj had him brought out in the hall that he might again see him in the orange cloth. It seemed to give him the greatest pleasure to have him dressed as a *Sannyasin.*

"Sri Ramakrishna used to explain that among his disciples there were certain ones who were his '*Antar-anga,*' that is, who formed, as it were, his vital organs; they would always come with him whenever he incarnated. These were Narendra, Rakhal, Baburam and Niranjan. He always predicted that Niranjan would not survive him long and he did not. Of these *Antar-anga,* he said that Naren would be the one who would understand him most fully.

"This understanding did not come at once, however. Again and again doubt of the Master rose and Naren would shed bitter tears over his lack of faith. Instead of reproaching him, Sri Ramakrishna would weep with him and strive to comfort him. Still doubt came. Even at the end, only a short time before Gurumaharaj left the body, it rose, but found no expression. Gurumaharaj caught the thought, however, and he repeated three times with great emphasis: 'He who was Rama, He who was Krishna, has now become Ramakrishna.' The threefold repetition indicated the unquestionable truth of the statement."

Narendra was not the first disciple to join Sri Ramakrishna. Two others preceded him—Rakhal and Latu. They came to the Master from widely-diverging points in the social order. Rakhal was the son of a rich *Zemindar* or land-holder, Latu was a servant; Rakhal grew up in luxury and ease, Latu in poverty and toil; Rakhal had careful schooling, Latu could neither read nor write. Yet this simple boy, serving in humble capacity in a rich man's home, was so open to Sri Ramakrishna's transforming influence that in a few weeks after he came to live at the Temple, he attained superconscious vision. In later years he developed also a remarkable power to expound the Scriptures, although he was unable to read them and had to have some one read them for him.

Latu came to Sri Ramakrishna in this wise. The gentleman whose servant he was, Ram Chandra Dutt, often sent offerings to Sri Ramakrishna and Latu carried them to the Temple for him. Always he lingered near the Master as if reluctant to leave him. Sri Ramakrishna observed his devout, reverent bearing and divining behind it unusual spiritual aptitude, one day he said to Ram Chandra: "You are asking continually to do something for me. Send Latu to serve me."

From that time Latu remained at Dakshineswar and served Sri Ramakrishna faithfully and lovingly. He seemed to understand his Master's every need and gave him the tender care a mother might give her little child, scolding him when he did not eat enough or was too indifferent to his own welfare. He squatted near him while he took his meal and watched beside him while he slept. The disciple Sasi told me that he learned to serve by seeing Latu.

The Master felt a strong protecting love for this lowly disciple, but Latu would never acknowledge that he was among the chosen. When I met him first I said to him that I was peculiarly glad to meet him because I knew he was especially dear to Sri Ramakrishna. His answer flashed back almost like a rebuke: "My Master loved all equally." He did not mean to be sharp or discourteous, but he could not bear to have an ordinary human trait like partiality attributed to that one who in his eyes was far beyond all human limitations.

Rakhal, the next disciple to come, was like Sri Ramakrishna's own son. He slept in the same room with him, sometimes in the same bed; and he dared show a greater familiarity with him than any of the other disciples. When Sri Ramakrishna would be sitting on the floor, he would come up behind him, put his arms round his neck and rock him back and forth. The others never sat in the Master's presence unless bidden to do so, or spoke unless spoken to. Not that the Master exacted this of them, it was the spontaneous expression of the reverent awe they felt.

Rakhal had no lack of reverence. To Sri Ramakrishna he was always a little boy. Sri Ramakrishna would say when a devotee brought him an offering of food: "Give it to Rakhal. Feeding him is the same as feeding me. I eat through him." Sometimes he would feed him from his own plate. Rakhal rarely left the Master's side. He accompanied him whenever he went to different houses in Calcutta; he sat near him when the Master received visitors at the Temple.

Despite this tender intimacy now and then a shadow of doubt fell across Sri Ramakrishna's mind. Did Rakhal look upon him as a real father? One night he had the proof. Rakhal was sleeping in his room. Sri Ramakrishna was thirsty and asked the boy to bring him some water. Rakhal gave a grunt of refusal, turned over on his mat and went to sleep. Sri Ramakrishna exclaimed with delight: "I see now that he really thinks of me as his own father;" and he went about telling everyone of the incident.

Whenever Sri Ramakrishna was asked how a man would act who had gone beyond the three

Gunas (that is, had transcended material bondage) he always replied 'Like Rakhal.' The disciple Sasi once said to me: "The self in Rakhal was utterly annihilated. Any one whom he takes under his guidance is saved." Sri Ramakrishna often declared that Rakhal was a *Nityasiddha* (born perfect) and he guarded his unworldliness and ready renunciation with jealous care. He would say to him: "My son I would rather have you throw yourself into the Ganges than do anything unworthy for the sake of money or worldly gain. Only a pure soul who is free from worldliness can love God truly and keep the mind fixed on Him alone."

There was still another disciple who joined Sri Ramakrishna about this time. His name was Gopal Sen, but he was always called Gopaldada, Gopal the elder brother. Throughout, in speaking of the disciples, I have retained their boyhood names, because Sri Ramakrishna used no other. Even to-day in the intimate circle of the religious household these names continue to be spoken with the term of respect "Maharaj" attached. The spiritual names were given after the Master's passing by Narendra when he was made leader of the youthful band. Rakhal was called "Maharaj." Narendra suggested the title one day when the boyish disciples were playing together. The boys seized upon the idea with delight and the Master's sanctioning pleasure, when he was told of it, converted the suggestion into a habit. Rakhal came to live at the Temple before any of the others.

Gopaldada was a cloth merchant and much the senior of the younger men who gathered round Sri Ramakrishna. Stricken by the loss of his wife, he went to the *Paramahamsa* at the Temple for comfort. At first he saw little that was remarkable in him, but gradually Sri Ramakrishna's subtle atmosphere of godliness and guileless wisdom enveloped him and wove a spell about his heart, drawing him away from his grief and his worldly occupation.

His business training had given him an unusual sense of order, exactitude and industry. Sri Ramakrishna often held him up as an example and even at an advanced age he was more active than the young men of the group—gardening, training the young boys in book-keeping, doing many things, and despite the intense Indian heat taking a long walk every day.

It is not my intention to carry the account of the disciples to the end. It is only as their lives mingle with the Master's life and form a part of his immediate environment that they have a place in the present narrative.

OTHER DISCIPLES

Baburam was the next disciple to come to the Master. He was a school friend of Rakhal and knew that he went to Dakshineswar to visit a *Sadhu* there. His elder brother had spoken of the same *Sadhu* and he himself had seen him in Calcutta. One day he asked Rakhal about him and Rakhal proposed that they go out and spend the night at the Temple.

Sri Ramakrishna received Baburam with great loving-kindness. They found many points of contact in places and people and the Master's welcome grew even warmer when he discovered that Baburam's sister was the wife of Balaram Babu, a close householder devotee. For his own sake also was Baburam's reception a cordial one. He was tall and slender and unusually handsome, with a glowing personality. His heart was full of tenderness and sweetness and drew everyone to him.

"He was so impressed by Sri Ramakrishna that he wanted his mother also to know him, so he and his brother took her to Dakshineswar," the disciple Sarat told me. "She sat near the Master with her veil closely drawn. Seeing this, Baburam went to her and said: 'Mother why do you keep your veil over your face? Do you not know that this is not an ordinary man. Would you veil yourself before God?' The mother replied simply: 'Is he God? He seems just like a man to me. He is very beautiful to look at, no doubt, and I love to hear the words he speaks, but he appears just like a man.' Nevertheless she remained at Dakshineswar for several days and afterwards she became a great devotee of Gurumaharaj."

This incident reveals Baburam's feeling towards the Master. He came more and more frequently to the Temple and finally begged to be accepted as a disciple. He grew rapidly so close to the heart of Sri Ramakrishna that he was accounted one of the *Antar-anga* or "vital organs." Niranjan, another of the same inner group, followed Baburam in order of succession. He possessed greater personal beauty even than Baburam, being very tall with broad shoulders, wonderfully poised head and majestic carriage. I saw in India a picture of him seated in meditation and it looked like the bronze statue of some Deity.

He was eighteen years of age when he had his first meeting with Sri Ramakrishna and at the moment he was somewhat interested in spiritualism. Learning of this, Sri Ramakrishna said to him: "If you spend your time thinking of ghosts, you will grow to be like one. If you spend the same time thinking on God, you will become God-like. Which seems to you better?" Niranjan needed no argument, Sri Ramakrishna himself was to his mind a supreme reason for choosing the religious life and God above all else.

Niranjan did not survive his Master very long.

A devotee who was present told me of his last visit to Holy Mother, as Sri Ramakrishna's widow was called. It discloses his loving impulsive nature. He made no mention of the approaching end, but he was like a tearful child clinging to its mother. He insisted that Holy Mother do everything for him, even feed him, and he wanted only what she had made ready for his meal. When the time came for him to leave her, reluctantly he threw himself at her feet, weeping tears of tender sadness; then silently he went away, knowing that he would never see her again.

She loved all the disciples as her own children, but Yogin, the disciple who joined Sri Ramakrishna after Niranjan, was specially dear to her heart. He was the son of an orthodox Brahmin and observed all the traditional rites of his caste. Even as a child he was unusually thoughtful and meditative, spending his time in religious reflection and study. He lived in the village of Dakshineswar and was in the habit of walking in the garden of the Temple and bathing at its *Ghat*. Thus he came in contact with Sri Ramakrishna. The Master knew members of his family and a friendly relation was established at once.

Yogin came daily to the Temple. He grew more and more detached, more abstracted in thought, less interested in worldly affairs. His whole soul was moving towards God. The family made drastic efforts to draw him back into practical life, but all their attempts were ineffectual. At last they were obliged to let him go his way. He began to spend the entire day and sometimes the night with the Master, until at last the spirit of renunciation swept away everything and left him with but one desire—to give himself utterly.

Yogin had touched the Brahmo influence, but only lightly. The next to follow, Sasi and Sarat, were strongly imbued with it. They were cousins and together they had become members of Keshab's Samaj. Sasi himself gave me this account of his going to the Temple: "I had a desire to see the *Paramahamsa* at Dakshineswar because Keshab Chandra Sen had spoken of him in such high terms, so one day I went with fifteen or twenty other boys. I was then reading for F. A. (First Arts) and the others were all preparing for their matriculation. Being the eldest of the band, the conversation was addressed to me.

"I talked a great deal that first day, but never again. After I had listened to Ramakrishna, I had nothing more to say. I did not have to talk. Often I would go to him with my mind full of some doubt which I wished him to clear away; but when I reached the Temple I would find his room full of people and would feel very much disappointed. As soon as he saw me he would say: 'Come in; sit down. Are you doing well?' Then he would return to his subject, but invariably he would take up the very doubt that was troubling my mind and would clear it away completely.

"He was extremely fond of ice. One day when it was very hot I walked from Calcutta to Dakshineswar (six miles) to carry him a piece of ice wrapped in paper. It was just noontime and the sun's rays were so strong that they blistered my body. When Gurumaharaj saw me, he began to say 'Oh! Oh!' as if he was in pain. I asked him what was the matter and he said that as he looked at my body, his own began to burn. Strange to say the ice did not melt at all on the way."

Sasi made no compromises in his discipleship. He was devotion embodied. Once at the Temple when he was studying Urdu in order to read the Sufi poets in the original, the Master called him three times before he heard. When he came Sri Ramakrishna asked what he had been doing and Sasi told him. "If you forget your duties for the sake of study, you will lose all your devotion," Sri Ramakrishna remarked quietly. Sasi sensed the deeper significance of his words. He had bigger things to learn. He took his Persian books and threw them into the Ganges.

He had heard of the beauty of Sufi poetry from Naren. He and Naren and Sarat were inseparable. They spent long days together at the Temple and their discussions and conferences were unending. Sasi told me of one night when the three walked back from Dakshineswar together. Reaching Calcutta they could not bear to separate, so Naren went home with Sarat and Sasi. The two cousins lived under the same roof. Then Sarat and Sasi walked to Naren's house. Still the discussion was not finished, so Naren came back with Sasi and Sarat and Sarat and Sasi returned with Naren. This kept up until two in the morning, then none of the boys dared go home. While they were debating what to do, an old house collapsed in the neighborhood. They ran to the rescue of the occupants and in the excitement no one noticed their return.

Disciples continued to come,—Hari, Gangadhar, Tarak, Kali, Tulasi, Subodh. Kali was a schoolmate of Baburam. Hari knew Sasi and Sarat, Gangadhar was a friend of Harinath, so one boy brought another. Kali's father was a successful teacher of English. Tulasi lived not far from Balaram Babu's house and it was here he first saw the Master. Tarak's home was not far from Dakshineswar and although he met with some opposition from his family, he came more and more frequently to the Temple. Sri Ramakrishna showed him great favor which kindled in his heart such spiritual yearning that worldly life could hold him no longer.

Gangadhar was the youngest in years. He was only fourteen when he first met Sri Ramakrishna, but he did not join him until somewhat later. He lived for a time with a *Sadhu*. It was on his return that with his friend Harinath he sought to enter into closer relations with the *Paramahamsa* at Dakshineswar. He was very conservative in his religious habit and careful about food and associates. The Master gave him various disciplines to correct this rigidity, but Gangadhar remained always an uncompromising monist. He did not know Sanskrit, but he committed to memory in Sanskrit long passages from Sankaracharya's monistic writings and would stand up and recite them with eloquent ardor. He has proved one of the most productive and useful of the Master's workers.

Only a few of the disciples lived at the Temple. The majority remained in their homes and came and went as they could. Most of them were university or college students and their parents watched with displeasure their growing habit of spending their days at Dakshineswar instead of in the class-room. Interest in studies grew less and less. As a result some of the boys failed to take their degree. After the Master's passing, however, they resumed their college work and made amends for their neglect.

Sri Ramakrishna did not give formal *Sannyas* (higher initiation) to any of his disciples. Formalism and calculation were not in his nature. He moved wholly by the impulsion of the Divine Mother's will. His actions were always spontaneous and unplanned. He gave the first initiation to his boys, thus laying the foundation of their spiritual life; but he left the second to be given by Naren, who became the leader of the group after the Master was gone.

Among the devotees, however, was a cloth-merchant. One day Sri Ramakrishna requested him to dye a bolt of cloth orange-color and bring it to him. When it was brought, he told the boys to put the cloth on, take begging bowls and go out to beg for him. This was his simple way of making them *Sannyasins.* He needed no rite or ceremonial. The spirit of renunciation wound itself about them with the orange cloth and bound them to holy self-denial for all time. The fire of the Master's word, the purifying power of his touch, were sufficient consecration.

How they passed their days is told in these words by the disciple Sasi: "It was only on Sunday that there was a crowd at the Temple; on other days Gurumaharaj was left alone with his few chosen ones. Not every one could stay with him, only those whom he chose to have. And why did he keep them? In order that in one night he might make them perfect. Just as a goldsmith gives shape to a lump of gold, so he would mould them so that their whole life would be changed and they could never forget the impression he had stamped on them.

"He possessed the peculiar power to discern

at once whether a man was fit or not. Sometimes people would come and want to stay with him but he would see that they were not fit and he would tell them with child-like frankness, 'You would better go home.' When now and then there would be a feast and Gurumaharaj would be sitting with his disciples, a man would sometimes come who was not really good but who by sitting with him wanted to appear good; at once Gurumaharaj would make him out and would say: 'Here is a man who is not pure. He will spoil my children.' Without hesitation he would send him away.

"When he was alone with his special disciples, they would sing and talk and play together. If a visitor came, he would tell him: 'Go and have a bath, eat something and rest awhile.' Then about two o'clock he would begin to talk and he would go on teaching for five or six hours continuously. He would not know when to stop.

"Sometimes Gurumaharaj would wake at four in the morning and he would call the disciples who were sleeping in his room saying: 'What are you all doing? Snoring? Get up, sit on your mat and meditate.' Sometimes he would wake up at midnight, call them and make them spend the whole night singing and praising the name of the Lord."

METHODS OF TRAINING

Sri Ramakrishna was a gentle disciplinarian. He could be stern, even awe-inspiring; but most often he was like an indulgent mother who asks of her children only to be strong and well and happy-hearted. As the mother pins up the children's frocks, bares their feet and tells them to run and play, taking on herself the responsibility of tears and stains, so he assumed the care of salvation for all who sought his protecting guidance, demanding from them nothing but joyousness and trust.

The famous Bengali dramatist, Girish Chandra Ghose, once asked him what he should do to attain liberation. Sri Ramakrishna replied: "Take the name of the Lord three times a day." Girish protested that he might not remember. "Take the Lord's name twice a day then," was Sri Ramakrishna's counsel. "That too I may forget," Girish answered. "Try to repeat it once a day," Sri Ramakrishna replied. "Even that I cannot promise," Girish declared. "Then give yourself up to me and I will look to your salvation," Sri Ramakrishna rejoined.

His great brooding love led him to demand a minimum of effort from others. He had been relentless in his own searchings, sparing himself in nothing, but having attained the ultimate, he was ready to share his gains with the world. He had no wish to keep anything for his own. "If you will practise even one-sixteenth part of what I have practised," he said to his disciples, "you will surely reach the goal." That sixteenth part of individual striving, however, was essential. He could not impose realization as one pastes a picture on a page. Some one said to him once: "You have the power by a touch to make a man perfect, why do you not do it?" "Because if I did, the man would not be able to keep perfection. He must grow to it and be ready to take it," was the answer.

There were no flagellations, no grim self-denials or self-torturings in Sri Ramakrishna's scheme of development. "His method was peculiar," the disciple Sasi explained to me one day. "He did not tell a man to give up. On the contrary, he would say: 'Go on, my children, enjoy all you wish. The Divine Mother has given this universe for your enjoyment. But as you enjoy remember always that it does not come from yourself, but out of the Mother's bounty. Never forget Her in your pleasure, but always recognize that it is from Her.' In this way, by making the man mindful of the Mother, he gradually lost all taste for the pleasures of the senses."

I had personal knowledge of one such instance. A prominent Indian gentleman, representative of an important English business firm, had learned from his British associates to take too much wine. When he came under Sri Ramakrishna's influence, he confessed his weakness and asked Sri Ramakrishna if he would have to give up drinking, should he become his disciple. "Why should you give up?" Sri Ramakrishna exclaimed. "It is not necessary; but when you drink, always offer your glass of wine to the Lord." The son of the gentleman related to me that his father from that time never drank without saying a prayer. As time went on he thought more and more of God and less and less of the wine until he lost all taste for it.

Sri Ramakrishna's way of breaking a detrimental habit is shown by this story which he himself was fond of telling. A man went to a doctor and asked what he could do to overcome a deeply rooted opium habit. The doctor told him not to try to give it up, but to weigh his daily ration of opium with a piece of chalk as the measuring weight in the other scale. Each day before weighing he was to draw a line on the floor with the chalk. At the end of six months the chalk was gone, the opium ration had been reduced to nothing and the habit was broken. This was the method Sri Ramakrishna applied invariably.

"He never told us that anything was wrong," the disciple Sasi said again. "On the contrary, he used to say: 'Go and have a good time. The responsibility will be mine.' He knew there was nothing wrong in the pleasures of the world; that by tasting them his children would come to realize their worthlessness and be satisfied only with higher pleasures. He was not merely the helper of the good. He was also the helper of the wicked. He tolerated and loved both. He wanted his children to be always happy; and if one of us came with the least shadow on his face, he could not bear that and he would at once scold us."

There was no form of selfishness which called forth a sharper rebuke from Sri Ramakrishna than gloominess. He used to say that a child of the all-blissful Divine Mother had no right or cause to be other than blissful; that man owed it to the world to keep cheerful. If he could not show a smiling face to his fellowmen, he should shut himself up alone until he could. Yet Sri Ramakrishna was never harsh or hard in his judgment.

"He never condemned any man. He was ready to excuse everything," the disciple Sasi declared. "He used to tell us that the difference between man and God was this: If a man failed to serve God ninety-nine times, but the hundredth time served Him with even a little love, God forgot the ninety-nine times he had failed and would say: 'Oh! my devotee served me so well to-day.' But if a man serves another man well ninety-nine times and the hundredth time fails in his service, then man will forget the ninety-nine good services and say: 'That rascal failed to serve me one day.' So Sri Ramakrishna, if there is the least spark of good in any one, sees only that and overlooks all the rest.

"Just by looking at a man he could tell what he was fitted for. If he saw that he was falsely leading a religious life, he would say to him: 'Go and get married.' If he saw that a man was ready to renounce, he would not ask him directly to give up, but he would direct his mind in such a way that the man would of his own accord give up. He used to say that by seeing even one corner of a man's toe, he could make out just what sort of man he was.

"At one time there was a very poor boy who used to come almost daily to Sri Ramakrishna, but the Master would never take any of the food he brought. We did not know why. Finally one day Sri Ramakrishna said: 'This poor fellow comes here because he has a great desire to be rich. Very well, let me taste a little of what he has brought,' and he took a small quantity of the food. The boy's condition began to improve immediately and to-day he is one of the most prosperous men of Calcutta.

"He had the power by a word or a touch to transform the whole life and character. Something went with the word or touch which lent it impelling power. There was a certain young man who came often to Sri Ramakrishna. He was a great devotee, but being the son of a rich man, he had been brought up in luxury and his body was as soft as butter—beautiful to look at, but with no strength or endurance in it. One day in speaking of him to some one, our Master said: 'He is a good boy and has true devotion, but his body is against him. With that body he can never hope to do much in this life.' The boy overheard the remark and at once he began a regular course of training, which in two years made his muscles like iron.

"There was another boy who came often to Dakshineswar to see Gurumaharaj. One day he took him into the Temple and touching his heart, gave him a vision of the Divine. Afterwards he explained that the boy would not be able to realize God in this life, but he wished to show him what he would attain in his next birth, that he might be encouraged to struggle for it. I remember once he took the *Karma* (difficulties) of a certain devotee on himself and suffered from a serious bodily disorder for six months."

Sometimes Sri Ramakrishna's method of correcting a wrong condition or tendency was wholly silent and even casual, without word or touch. The youngest of the immediate disciples—a mere lad of fifteen or sixteen, had formed the habit of taking snuff. When Sri Ramakrishna learned of it, he did not refer to it in any way, but he invited the disciple to spend the day with him at the Temple. The boy came bringing with him his snuff-box tucked away in hiding. As the hours passed Sri Ramakrishna kept him continuously busy. Again and again the boy tried to slip away behind a bush or tree and snatch a pinch of snuff, but always at that very moment Sri Ramakrishna would call him for some pressing service. Not once was he able to satisfy his desire and when the day was over, to his surprise he found all craving for snuff was gone.

A curious incident took place at the Temple which illustrated Sri Ramakrishna's subtle and unusual manner of helping and sustaining his devotees. The disciple Sasi told me of it thus: "There was a famous wrestler in Bengal, whom no one was able to defeat. He kept sending out challenges everywhere, but not one dared take them up. Finally he received an answer from an unknown person and a day was set for the contest.

"On the morning of the day a silent slender man appeared at the Temple and remained constantly with Gurumaharaj. Wherever Sri Ramakrishna went the stranger followed like his shadow, walking always just behind him with bent head and clasped hands as if in worship. He refused to touch food or water. Gurumaharaj's behavior also was singular. After his bath in the morning he asked to put on the short cloth of an athlete and to be adorned with garlands. At the hour for the wrestling match he went to the place and walked straight to the centre of the arena, followed by the strange man. Then he took his seat among the on-lookers and the contest began.

"When people saw the small lean man beside the giant Bengali wrestler, everyone began to laugh; and the wrestler himself did not want to begin the fight. At the first round he threw him, then once again he said: 'It is better to stop. I shall merely hurt you for nothing.' But the stranger rose and advanced on his adversary, whom he threw with perfect ease again and again. At last he offered to let him off, but the wrestler refused to admit that he was defeated, so without a word the man seized his hand and crushed it by one grip. Gurumaharaj explained afterward that this man was a great devotee and his phenomenal strength was altogether the result of his intense devotion."

Sri Ramakrishna had no fixed rules which he applied indiscriminately, no rigid set of practices or exercises which he gave to all alike. His methods were elastic and pliable to an indefinite degree. They took shape according to the need of the person. On one disciple he enjoined the strictest vegetarian diet; to another he gave permission to eat whatever he chose, saying that he had a fire burning within him which would consume all impurities. Still another who had an unbending prejudice against animal food, he sent to the bazar to buy some meat; and when the disciple brought him the meat with the juice running down through his fingers on to his fresh white *Dhoti,* he commended him for his ready obedience, told him he need not eat the meat and let him go to purify himself by a bath in the Ganges.

His own attitude of mind towards diet he voiced in these words spoken to a group of disciples: "He who eats meat and keeps his mind firmly fixed on God is a vegetarian; and he who takes nothing but vegetable food and keeps his mind turned towards his selfish concerns and his worldly affairs is a meat-eater." He himself was most abstemious. A little soup or a little thick gruel (*Payasam*) constituted a meal for him. If, however, he cared little for food, it gave him great delight to see others eat and enjoy. The offerings of choice fruits and sweets which were brought him by devotees he would save for Naren or Rakhal; or he would carry a sweet-meat to the school gate in Calcutta and wait there to give it to Purna or another of his boys as he came from class. Now and then when the boys were at the Temple, he would keep them for the evening meal; and as they ate on the verandah outside his door, he would hover around them with motherly solicitude, eager to have them eat well and wisely.

Sometimes before the meal he would send them to meditate under the banyan tree, then he would follow quickly after, bringing mats for them to sit on, lest the brick platform round the tree might be damp. Occasionally he would turn from mother into playmate and propose a game of leap-frog. Or he would amuse them with stories and mimicry. Spiritual life with him was full of gaiety and laughter. The disciple Sasi in speaking of this said:—

"Religion as Sri Ramakrishna taught it was never vague or dismal. It went to the man where he was and lifted him up. It was not like an eagle which soars high in the air and calls to the tortoise, 'Come up here.' Can the tortoise ever hope to rise to the eagle? No, it can only say, 'If you will come and lift me up, then I can go up there.' So Sri Ramakrishna in his teaching came down and carried the man up by degrees. It gave him new hope and courage.

" 'God may come at any time,' he would say; 'but this need not frighten us. When the king wishes to visit one of his servants, he knows the servant will not have soft cushions and the proper things to receive him, so the day before he comes he sends servants to cleanse everything and prepare for his reception. Similarly God, before He comes to the heart, sends His servants to make it ready for His coming. And who are those servants? Purity, chastity, humility, loving-kindness. Or again, as in the east the red glow in the sky tells us that the sun is about to rise, so just by looking at a man, one can tell whether God will come soon to him.'

"What keeps us from attaining to God now? some one asked. Sri Ramakrishna's answer was: 'The ego. The ego is the greatest obstacle in man's path. It is his greatest enemy. To be rid of ego means *Mukti* or freedom. It is not easy to conquer the ego, but if you cannot conquer it, let it remain as the servant of God.' "

WOMEN DISCIPLES

There were three women disciples whose service was specially pleasing to Sri Ramakrishna. He was always happy to take food from their hands or to let them serve him in any way. One was Balaram Babu's wife, who was also the sister of the disciple Baburam; the others were Gopal-ma and the wife of Navagopal Ghose. Gopal-ma came to him in 1884. She was then nearly sixty years of age. I heard the story of her coming from the disciple Sasi and shall repeat it as he spoke it.

"Gopal-ma was left a widow at the age of eight," he said. "She began her life of devotion even then and always thought of herself as the mother of the Baby Krishna. Whatever she did, she did for her Gopala (the name of Baby Krishna). If she cleaned her room, she thought that it was Gopal's room which she was cleaning; if she prepared a meal, she did it for Gopala; so she grew up with the idea of Gopala firmly fixed in her mind.

"One day she was cooking as usual, but the fire would not burn, the wood was heavy with moisture, and there was an adverse wind which blew the smoke into her eyes. Finally when the bit of rice and curry was done and she was about to pour it out on the leaf, the same adverse wind blew away the leaf. She began to scold the Lord for making everything so bad for Gopala. As she was talking, a little boy brought back the leaf, held it out flat on the ground until she had put the food on it, then disappeared.

"She began to feed her unseen Gopala; but suddenly she asked herself who that little boy was and she realized that it was Gopala himself. From that moment she was grief-stricken. All day and night she kept crying, 'Where is my Gopala?' 'Where is my Gopala?' She could not sleep or eat. Only at night would she prepare a little food for Gopala. Nothing could comfort her and everyone thought that she had really become mad.

"One day some friends, thinking to distract her mind, told her that they were going to see a great soul called Ramakrishna at the Temple of Dakshineswar and asked if she would not come with them. She consented. As it was contrary to the Scriptures to go to a *Sadhu* empty-handed, she collected the little rice, *dal* (pulses) and curry stuff she had and joined them. But when they reached the Temple the others had such rich presents of fruit, flowers and other things to offer that she was ashamed of her little bundle and, hiding it, she took her place in a far corner of the room.

"As soon as the other presents were offered, to her great surprise, Sri Ramakrishna walked back to where she sat and said to her: 'I am feeling very hungry, can you not give me something to eat?' 'Oh Sir,' she replied, 'What can I do?' I am a poor woman. I have no money. What can I get for you?' 'But what is that?' he asked, pointing to her little bundle. With shame she opened it and showed him. 'Oh,' he said, 'will you not cook for me? The kitchen is right over there.' And he himself took her and showed her where it was.

"Shyly she began to prepare the food, thinking all the while: 'How can I offer it to him! I have no *Ghee* (clarified butter), nothing to make it tasty.' But just as it was ready he came eagerly to inquire if it was done and she laid it before him. 'You would better feed me,' he said to her. She mixed the rice and curry and as she put the first mouthful into his mouth, she saw her Gopala. 'You are my Gopala,' she exclaimed. Sri Ramakrishna then finished the food, declaring that he had never eaten anything so good; and to every one he kept saying: 'I have tasted real nectar today.'

"From that moment Gopal-ma's grief vanished and she was perfectly happy. Occasionally she would come to Dakshineswar with some rice and *dal* and vegetables and a few pieces of firewood, cook for Sri Ramakrishna and go away content. The rest of the time she spent serving her Gopala at home and making *Japam* (repeating the name of the Lord).

"One day after Sri Ramakrishna had passed away, some of his disciples went to see her and found her room full of mosquitoes and other troublesome creatures. Although she did not appear to mind them and kept on repeating the name of the Lord, it distressed them to see her in such discomfort, so next day one of the disciples carried her a mosquito curtain. That night when she sat down to repeat the Name, she found her mind constantly wandering to the curtain, thinking whether a cockroach or a rat might not be eating off a corner of it.

"Seeing this, she said: 'What! This wretched curtain thus to take my mind away from my Gopala!' And without ado she made it up into a bundle and sat down again to her devotions with the mosquitoes all about her.

"The next morning we were just getting up at the *Math* (monastery) when Gopal-ma appeared. She had walked all the way (at least five miles) and must have started at three o'clock. She laid the bundle down. 'What is it?' some one asked. 'It is the curtain you gave me yesterday. It takes my mind away from God. I don't want it,' was her answer; and nothing could persuade her to take it back."

Yogin-ma and many other lady devotees also went frequently to Dakshineswar and would sometimes spend two or three days there with Holy Mother, sleeping in the small room on the first floor of the Concert House. On occasions there would be eight or ten crowded into the small space, with no windows, only an oval opening like an eye at the back and the wooden door in front. Holy Mother used to cook under the stairs on the verandah outside, which was then railed in. Sri Ramakrishna would take curries made by any of his lady devotees—the only thing he was strict about was rice. He would not take rice from any other than a Brahmin in order not to offend against tradition. He liked very much the curries made by Yogin-ma.

She told me that when they would catch the first glimpse of the dome of the Dakshineswar Temple from the river, they would grow so impatient to arrive and see the Master that they would feel as if they wanted to jump down from the boat and run over the water. Sri Ramakrishna used to tell them they could come in a boat, but he did not like them to return by the river after nightfall, so, often they would walk the long way back, reaching home at ten or eleven o'clock.

From the disciple Sarat I learned that when a devotee first came to Sri Ramakrishna, the Master would go frequently to his house at the outset in order to increase his devotion. So it was that he went to Yogin-ma's house, to the house of Golap-ma or to other houses in Calcutta. These visits were occasions of great rejoicing. Sometimes fifty or sixty ladies would congregate to listen to the Master and he would talk to them in his simple informal way for several hours.

In one house to which he went often there was

a lawless youth who resented the special privilege accorded this unknown *Sadhu*. The man was a fraud, he declared, merely pretending to be a *Sadhu* in order to gain access to the inner quarters of the house; and he determined to get rid of him. He proposed to his associates that they give him a good lesson to frighten him away. Not long after, Sri Ramakrishna came again to the house and the boys gathered in a room beside the entrance and awaited their opportunity. Sri Ramakrishna was taken at once to the inner court where forty or fifty ladies were assembled.

Yogin-ma was one of those present and she told me that after the Master had talked for a while, suddenly he rose, left the room and walked hurriedly towards the outer court. After a time he returned and without comment resumed his teaching. Later they learned that he had gone straight to the room beside the entrance door where the boys were watching for him and, laying his hand on the arm of the leader of the band, he had said in quiet tones: "So you mean to give me a good thrashing, do you?" The boy, she said, started, turned and saw Sri Ramakrishna. As he looked into the gentle eyes and at the smiling face, all his resentment melted away and a shadow of shame fell over him. He paused for a moment, then raising his arm with clenched fist, he called out: "If any boy here dares to lay a hand on this man, I will give him a sound beating."

Sri Ramakrishna went back to the inner court and remained for more than an hour. When he came out again he found the boy standing by the carriage. He helped Sri Ramakrishna in, closed the door, and ran beside the carriage for a long distance. When Sri Ramakrishna protested that he was tiring himself unnecessarily, the boy explained that his companions, angry at the unexpected swing of events, might still try to carry out their plan and he wished to be near to protect him. From that day he was a staunch defender and admirer of Sri Ramakrishna. He did not come to the Temple as others did, but he lost all the lawlessness which had marked his nature and his whole life was remoulded.

Yogin-ma was a very dear disciple of the Master. She possessed exceptional beauty and an uplifted dignity which told of rare nobility of character. She was the wife of a rich *Zemindar* and when she knew Sri Ramakrishna first she was living in luxurious estate. By a foolish act of her husband their fortune was swept away in a night. She refused to have recourse to law to regain it, declaring that poverty would teach her husband what he had not learned from riches and she herself was content to have little. She gave herself up with more ardor to her spiritual life and multiplied her visits to the Master, serving him with ever-increasing devotion.

In contrast to Yogin-ma's majestic personality

was that of the simple, modest wife of Mahendra Nath Gupta. She had no thought beyond her home and her children, yet Sri Ramakrishna gave her the same attention that he gave to the more learned and important. He even rebuked Mahendra Nath sharply at their first meeting because he spoke of her as good but ignorant. "You think that she is ignorant and that you are very wise?" he exclaimed in a questioning tone.

She brought all her household difficulties to Sri Ramakrishna as she might carry them to a mother, and he would sit for two or three hours at a time talking over with her the ailments of the children and the failings of the servants. She sought his advice about the best food to bring from the bazar, how she should discipline the children when they were naughty, and what she could do to make her husband more comfortable and happy. Sri Ramakrishna listened and answered with grave interest. He never showed the least impatience or inattention. Any one would have supposed that he himself was a housewife and mother.

Another earnest and faithful disciple was Golap-ma. Overwhelming grief at the loss of an only daughter carried her to the Master's feet. She found immediate consolation and strength to go bravely on her way. She lived not far from Yogin-ma and heard of Sri Ramakrishna through her. Gaur-ma, still another devotee, came to him through Balaram Babu. So one devotee made known to others the peculiar power and wisdom of the *Paramahamsa* of Dakshineswar.

Gaur-ma was a *Sannyasini* (a woman who has renounced and taken up the religious life). She paid frequent visits to the Temple and sometimes she would spend several days there, living with Holy Mother. Like Gopal-ma, occasionally she would prepare a meal for the Master, cooking it on the open hearth under the narrow adobe stairway on the curtained verandah of the Concert House.

There were many more women disciples—it is not possible to name them all. Sri Ramakrishna had a profound reverence for womanhood. To him God was primarily the Mother and woman was Her shrine. He saw in each woman the sanctified image of Divine Mother. Even the prostitute in the street had in his eyes something holy in her—the reflection of Divinity, he declared, can never be completely obscured. He used to say that this was the Divine Mother's age and woman must take a leading part in shaping the world's life. She would fulfill her high mission, he believed, however, not by denying her womanhood, but by glorifying it.

DEVOUT HOUSEHOLDERS

The distance of six miles from Calcutta to Dakshineswar seemed very long in the scorching heat of daylight hours and very lonely and dark by night; yet many disciples and devotees traversed it habitually on foot, some out of humility, some because they had not the money for carriage hire or boat fare. It hurt Sri Ramakrishna to see them arrive at the Temple hot and weary. He felt as if he himself had walked under the burning sun, as if his own feet were fevered from the long way. To save his chosen ones from such fatigue, he went as often as he could to Calcutta and let them gather round him there.

The house which he frequented most was that of Balaram Bose. It became at once a recognized centre for his work and has remained such ever since. It was in 1882 that Balaram Babu met the Master first. He was already firmly grounded in spiritual living. Although possessed of large estates and great wealth, his life was given wholly to God. For many years he had devoted the major portion of his time to devout meditation and Scriptural study. His heart and mind were ripe therefore for a new message and it was not difficult for him to recognize Sri Ramakrishna's superior power. He had heard of him and learned something of his teachings through articles in a publication edited by Keshab Chandra Sen. He was in his country home in Orissa at the time; but when he came to Calcutta for his daughter's marriage, he went to Dakshineswar to meet the Master.

This first visit was followed by numerous others. Balaram Babu's widow told me that it was their habit to spend Sunday with the Master always. They did not feel it fitting to drive to the Temple in a pretentious carriage with servants and clanking harness, yet to go on foot through the crowded streets of the city was contrary to the custom of Bengali ladies, who never go abroad except in palinquin or carriage. To solve the difficulty they rose at three in the morning and walked the six miles to the Temple while streets and roads were still empty of traffic and people. There they would wait until after eleven at night, when roads and streets were deserted once more, and walk the long way home again.

The whole family caught the fire of their devotion and shared in their fervor of spirit. I saw Balaram's mother-in-law, Baburam's mother. She was over ninety years of age, yet she still went on special occasions to visit the widowed Saradamani Devi. She was full of glowing ardor and expressed her devotion for the Master in many ways. One day she arrived at the Temple when the barber was cutting Sri Ramakrishna's hair. In India the barber goes to his customer. A curl fell from the shears on Sri Ramakrishna's lap. He picked it up and laughingly gave it to her. She took it home, put it in a silver box and preserved it with great reverence.

No one, however, in the devout household could surpass Balaram Babu in loyalty and unquestioning surrender. The disciple Sasi told me that Balaram had a little casket in which he kept a picture of the Master. It was his custom to waken at four in the morning, open his casket, stand up the picture and seated on his bed before it, spend a long time in prayer and meditation. When his life was ebbing and he was lying apparently unconscious, with closed eyes and helpless hands, exactly at four o'clock he reached for the casket, opened it, looked at the picture, and soon after passed away.

Another family that occupied a large place in Sri Ramakrishna's life was that of Navagopal Ghose. Navagopal's widow gave me this account of their first contact with the Master:—

"For a long time my husband had been searching for a *Sadhu* who could tell him how to realize God. He had begun to follow the instructions of one, when a friend said: 'Why do you waste your time on this man? Go to Dakshineswar; there you will find a *Paramahamsa* who will be able to clear all your doubts.' So one Sunday my husband and I went to Dakshineswar and saw Sri Ramakrishna. He received us most kindly and at once I felt that he was divine.

"For three years we did not return. My husband was practising certain *Sadhanas* (spiritual exercises) and he felt that he must finish them before he went to another teacher. Suddenly one day Thakur said to a visitor at the Temple: 'Some three years ago a man by the name of Navagopal Ghose came to see me with his wife. He has never been back since. Tell him I would like to see him.' After all those three years he recalled the name; and it was just at the moment when my husband had finished the *Sadhanas* that he sent for us. We went to him the following Sunday and from that time we went regularly every Sunday, going at ten in the morning and staying until ten at night."

A profound love for the Master became the governing force of Navagopal's life. It gave him keenest joy even to hear the Master's name and if a little boy in the street shouted it, he would throw him a coin. Soon the urchins realized this and as Navagopal walked each morning to his bath in the Ganges, a crowd of them would dance round him shouting at the top of their shrill little voices: "Jai Ramakrishna!" "Jai Ramakrishna!" "Jai Ramakrishna!" In reply he would scatter copper coins by handfuls. He was a man of wealth and owned a large house across the river from Calcutta, to which the Master came now and then. One of his sons has joined the work which has grown out of Sri Ramakrishna's life.

The wife too was an ardent devotee. The Master was specially fond of her. She herself related to me many incidents of her association with Sri Ramakrishna. Here are her own words: "When I would come he would send all the gentlemen out and remain talking with me alone. Once he asked me why I came, what I found in him to draw me so often to Dakshineswar. I replied: 'I cannot say. All I know is that that which made Prahlada forget his father, and Druva and others forget their parents, that I find here.'

"At Cossipore Garden he asked me again why I came to him. 'You have children, you have jewels and furniture. What then do you want in coming to me?' I replied: 'I do not want all these things. I come because I love you, because I want you. I want your blessing.' At once he went into *Samadhi* and as he came out of it he put his hand on my head and blessed me.

"A friend had told me I should make *Haribol* (repeat the name of the Lord) and I did so. But it caused great perplexity in my mind. 'Here I am calling upon Hari' (a name of the Lord) I said to myself, 'and yet I am told that one should seek salvation through the *Guru* (spiritual teacher) alone.' I went to Dakshineswar to see Sri Ramakrishna but before I could explain my trouble, he said to me: 'Guru and Hari are one.'

"One day he was coming to our house and a number of devotees had gathered to see him. When he arrived, he came straight upstairs and remained for some time talking with me. At that time I had a picture of Sri Krishna in my Shrine and I told him I was anxious to have a vision of Krishna. He went downstairs where all the Bhaktas were making *Sankirtan* (singing holy songs). They put a heavy garland round his neck which reached to his feet. At once he went into *Samadhi* and assumed the exact posture of Sri Krishna. All the devotees also went into a higher state of consciousness on seeing him. Later he asked me if I was now satisfied; I said I would like to see Radha by Sri Krishna's side. He smiled and replied: 'Oh, you will have to wait awhile for that.'

"At another time when he came to our house, he dressed himself in a *Sari* and put on bangles and jewels. As he sat down to eat the fruits and sweetmeats prepared for him, he talked and acted just like a young wife begging her husband for more jewels. He kept up the play for an hour or more. His power of mimicry was remarkable." This little incident was told me at Navagopal's house and his widow added: "You are sitting just where Thakur sat." Immediately I felt a usurper. We were on a high, broad, pillared verandah outside the door of the Shrine where the Master is daily honored in prayer and worship. He is still the guiding and impelling power in the life of the entire family.

The disciple Sasi told me of other devoted householder followers. "Babanath," he said, "was one of those whom Gurumaharaj spoke of as 'born perfect.' He also said that he and Narendra were affinities. But Babanath married. One day Gurumaharaj told me to go to him, saying I could learn much from him. I wondered why he should send me to a householder to learn; but when I saw Babanath I understood. As we sat talking of God, he went into meditation and tears of bliss and devotion poured down his cheeks. One could see that he was completely immersed in God.

"Purna was another beloved disciple of Sri Ramakrishna. He was brought to see him when he was only nine years old. 'Who am I?' Gurumaharaj asked the boy. Purna replied without a moment's hesitation, 'You are an incarnation of Deity.' Then Gurumaharaj asked him if he spent some time each day in thinking on God. The child replied that he often meditated and that when he did tears of joy streamed out of the outer corners of his eyes. Gurumaharaj always said of him that he had attained the highest stage of *Bhakti* (devotion). He loved him so much that he would now and then stand and wait at the gate of his school to give him some sweetmeat; and whenever he went to the house of any devotee in Calcutta he always asked that Purna be brought to him.

"Purna, however, was a rich man's son and they were afraid that he might be led away from them and become a *Sannyasin,* so they did not let him go willingly. One day Gurumaharaj, who was in Calcutta for the day, sent one of his disciples to bring him. The gatekeeper said he was sleeping and should not be disturbed; so the disciple came back without him. Then Gurumaharaj sent me and somehow I always managed to do whatever the Master asked of me. I went, pushed my way past the gate-keeper and went upstairs to the hall where Purna was lying asleep on the floor beside his brothers. I stooped down and pinched him gently. The boy woke up. I whispered to him why I had come and together we slipped out softly, told some story to the gate-keeper and ran away."

I continue to give the words of the disciple Sasi:—

"Suresh was an archskeptic and he laughed at the devotion which Balaram and some of his friends showed for the *Paramahamsa* at Dakshineswar. One day he accompanied Balaram to the Temple determined to confound him by his arguments against belief in God; but when he sat down in the presence of the simple *Sadhu,* his mind, so he told me afterwards, became a perfect blank. He could remember nothing of all the fine arguments he meant to present. Gurumaharaj spoke kindly to him as he did to everyone; then with apparent unconcern he began to tell him certain facts about his life. Suresh at once recognized his divine power, and falling at his feet, became his devoted follower. It was he who contributed much towards the maintenance of the disciples, when they came to live with their Master, and to provide meals for those who visited him at Dakshineswar.

"On one occasion when Gurumaharaj was talking with his disciples, he suddenly became entirely abstracted and for ten or fifteen minutes remained in that state. When he returned to outer consciousness, he explained: 'I have been with Suresh.' Suresh himself told later that he was sitting before the newly-set up image of the Divine Mother weeping that Gurumaharaj had not come to see it, for it was the first time at the *Durga-Puja* (Feast of Divine Mother) that he had remained away. Suddenly he saw Gurumaharaj before him, consoling him. He stayed with him for a little while and then went away, leaving his mind perfectly pacified."

Another skeptic who was transformed into an ardent devotee by the touch of Sri Ramakrishna's transmuting power was Girish Chandra Ghose or Girish Babu, as he was called in familiar intercourse. His gratitude knew no bounds. In giving expression to it one day, he exclaimed: "He who has enabled me to cross over the sea of this world and the no less terrible sea of skepticism, how can I repay or serve him? There is nothing in him I cannot worship."

At another time he said to me: "If I had known I was going to have such a wonderful *Guru* (spiritual teacher) I would have been even more wicked than I was, just for the joy of being forgiven. Sri Ramakrishna was like an indulgent mother to me always. He scolded his disciples sometimes, but he never scolded me. He came frequently to my house and was unfailing in his love towards me."

Girish Chandra Ghose was one of the most famous dramatists of modern Bengal. He wrote seventy remarkable dramas, some in a few hours, so impelling was the flow of his inspiration. He was also an able actor and manager of his own theatre. After he fell under the spell of Sri Ramakrishna's spiritual charm, he became a powerful channel for the Master's message. In every play he wrote there was invariably one character at least who set forth some phase of Sri Ramakrishna's many-sided personality and voiced some part of his teaching. So vital was the influence of his dramatic writings that not infrequently they would carry a man with irrisistible sweep out of the world into the silent seclusion of a mountain cave and vow him to meditation and holy study. I myself know of several such instances.

Girish Babu was by nature of devout mind, but unfortunate early association with religion in insincere aspects turned him away from it and threw him back on the theatre and all the outlawry which the stage represented at that time. He had read and heard of the *Paramahamsa* of Dakshineswar, but felt no desire to seek him out. One late afternoon, however, he learned that Sri Ramakrishna was at a house not far distant from his own. Out of curiosity he went to see him. He remained only a few minutes and came away still critical and unbelieving.

The impression made upon him was deeper than he realized and caused a violent upheaval in his soul. He began to wonder whether he was wise enough to direct his own life, whether he did not need a stronger hand to lead him. Yet where could he find such a hand? Whom could he accept as guide or *Guru?* The questioning grew so tormenting that he determined to appeal to Sri Ramakrishna for answer to it.

It so happened that Sri Ramakrishna had come that day to Balaram's house and divining the disturbance in Girish's mind, he sent for him. When Girish entered the long upper room where Sri Ramakrishna sat amid his devotees, the Master looked up with a loving smile and said quietly: "You have your *Guru.*" Still Girish was perplexed, so he went to the Temple. There as his eyes rested upon Sri Ramakrishna, he knew that Sri Ramakrishna alone could be his *Guru.*

From that instant his whole mode of thought and life was altered. He became unshakable in his confidence. Sri Ramakrishna said of him, "Girish's faith is like a rock, it cannot be overturned. It is rare in this world to find a man with such a faith." The Master went often to Girish's theatre and after the performance he would go behind the scenes. Girish told me that every member of the company down to the most obscure scene-shifter would watch for his coming and prostrate in humble reverence at his feet. The whole atmosphere of the theatre seemed transfused with a new purity and radiance.

The influence still persists and many of those who bowed before the Master then, now have a picture of him in their homes and at the close of day they hang a fresh garland round it and burn incense before it in devout remembrance.

DURGA CHARAN NAG

It was in 1880 that Durga Charan Nag first came under Sri Ramakrishna's holy influence. His father, Dindayal by name, was a pious orthodox Hindu, employed on a very modest salary in a large commercial firm of Calcutta. His mother passed away early and he was left to the care of his aunt, whose dying admonition, "Let your mind always dwell on God," gives us a picture of what must have been her living influence upon his younger years.

In those days schools were fewer than at present. There was only one in the vicinity of his home and that carried him through the third grade only. He begged his father to let him study in Calcutta, but there was not money enough. In some way, however, he learned that there were excellent schools in Dacca, ten miles distant from his village. With a handful of puffed rice for his noon-day meal he set out quietly on foot, made a tour of the Dacca schools and on his return in the evening said to his anxious foster-mother: "From to-morrow I am going to school in Dacca. Please have my meal ready by 8 o'clock." For fifteen months, in chilling rain or scorching heat, he trudged patiently the twenty miles, missing in all only two days.

At last the way opened for him to join his father and during a year and a half he studied at a Medical College in Calcutta. Later he worked with the well-known physician, Behari Lal Bhaduri, who gave him a careful training in Homeopathy. His success in his profession was immediate. He had a rare intuition in diagnosis and even as a student performed some remarkable cures. He refused, however, to charge any fixed fee for his services. If people chose to make him an offering, he would accept it, provided it was not more than he considered just. Once when he had saved from death a lady belonging to the household of his father's employer, Mr. Pal, they presented him with a silver casket filled with coins. He courteously declined to take it, begging that they give him twenty Rupees only (about seven dollars).

His father, out of all patience, exclaimed indignantly: "You will never succeed in your profession, I tell you, if you go on this way." The son replied humbly: "I cannot help it. What I believe to be wrong I cannot do, come what may. God is truth. Have you not always taught me to walk in the path of righteousness? The cost of the medicines did not amount to more than six Rupees (two dollars) and my fees for those seven days should not be over fourteen Rupees. How then could I accept more than twenty Rupees?"

Frequently instead of receiving, he gave money to his patients or made loans which were never repaid. There were times when he forgot to save enough even for his own meals. He would walk immense distances to visit the sick, especially if they chanced to be very poor. When he saw some suffering creature by the roadside he would carry him to his house and nurse him back to life. Once he found a man lying on the floor of his hut in a deplorable condition. He hurried home, took one of his own beds, carried it himself the long way and laid the poor man tenderly on it. Another time when the night was unusually sharp, he spread the warm woolen shawl he wore over a shivering patient; then in scanty clothing he kept vigil beside the sick bed under a roof half open to the sky.

He had no thought or fear for himself. When the plague was raging in Calcutta and the servant of a friend who had fled from the city was stricken with it, he nursed him with tireless devotion, carried him to the Ganges side when he begged to die there, held him in his arms until life was gone, then bore his body to the burning-ghat. The pain of others caused him acute suffering, his own troubled him but little.

Once he had been asked to come to Calcutta on business and eight Rupees and a blanket had been sent him for his journey. As he was buying his ticket, a poor woman with five ragged, hungry children appeared. His money and blanket went to her; then with only fifteen cents in his pocket he travelled on foot, swimming the streams and begging his food. It took him twenty-nine days to reach Calcutta.

It was not merely the wretched and destitute among human beings, however, whom he made his next of kin; dumb beasts and creeping things shared equally in his compassion. He could not injure the smallest thing that crawled. Rather than disturb a busy ant hill, he let the ants gnaw through a pillar of his verandah until it fell. When the fishmonger stopped before his door, he would buy the whole basketful of live fish and throw them back into a near by pond.

Even the cobra was to him a friend. Once a large one came into his garden and his wife begged him to kill it. "It is not the snake of the forest that does us harm," he said to her in rebuke; "it is the snake in the mind which kills a man." Then he spoke persuasively to the cobra and the villagers still tell how it followed him back to the jungle. "The outside world is the projection of your own mind," was his explanation. "As you give out to the world, so you receive back from it. It is like looking in a mirror. The reflection in the glass shows exactly the faces you make at it."

Despite his success, the demands of his profession grew more and more irksome to him as time went on. His mind too was troubled and full of unrest. A *Sadhu* (holy man) had said to him: "However great may be your faith and your love for God, unless you are properly initiated by a *Guru* (spiritual teacher) and carry on your spiritual practices under his guidance, you cannot attain God-vision." Day after day he sat on the bank of the Ganges, praying the Divine Mother to have pity on him and send him a *Guru.*

His friend Suresh had heard of the great Light of Dakshineswar through Keshab Chandra Sen. For two months he did not think to speak of it; but when at last he did so, Nagmahasaya, as he was often called, was filled with an irresistible desire to go at once to see the *Sadhu.* The next morning the two friends had their meal early and started for the Temple of Dakshineswar. It was the month of April and the sun was very hot, but they hurried along the parched road with such ardor that they went far beyond the Temple and had to retrace their steps. It was two o'clock when they reached the door of Sri Ramakrishna's room in the corner of the Temple enclosure.

They found a man seated there and asked him: "Sir, can you tell us where the *Paramahamsa* lives?" "Here," was the answer; "but to-day he is gone to Chandannagar." Sad-hearted and weary, they were turning away when they saw some one in the dim shadow of the room beckoning them to enter. It was Sri Ramakrishna himself. He gave them friendly welcome, explaining that it was Hazra's eccentricity to bar the door to strangers. They remained with him for several hours. While he was talking, he turned suddenly upon Nagmahasaya and asked: "Why do you look at me so intently?" "I had a great desire to see you and now I am satisfying myself," was Dr. Nag's child-like reply.

The next week they went again to the Temple. Through the intervening days thoughts of Sri Ramakrishna had burned like fire within Nagmahasaya. He came with feverish eagerness and as he entered the Master said: "You have done well to come again. I have been waiting for you." Then a little later he added: "No fear, my child, you have attained a very exalted state."

After that Nagmahasaya was a frequent visitor at Dakshineswar and grew to be one of the dearest among the Master's householder disciples. There was always a place for him close to the Master's feet; but so modest was he that at first he never went to the Temple on Sundays or holidays, feeling himself too insignificant to mingle with the great men who visited the Master on those special days. Yet later when they knew him, it was they who paid him honor.

He still struggled manfully to carry on his medical practice, feeling it his duty to please his father; but one day he overheard Sri Ramakrishna say to another devotee: "If the mind clings to tiny drops of medicine, how can it conceive of the vast universe?" That was sufficient. He went home, threw his medicine chest and his medical books into the Ganges, took a bath and began a new life. The more he saw of the Master, the stronger grew the spirit of renunciation within him;

but Sri Ramakrishna's unvarying answer to his pleadings was: "What harm is there in remaining a householder? Only keep the mind on God. Your life will set up a true ideal for householders. Men will wonder to see it."

Obediently Nagmahasaya returned to his home life. It was a bitter blow; but so rigidly did he abide by the Master's admonition that later, when several devoted friends asked to provide for him and those dependent on him that he might pass his remaining days under the sacred shadow of the Temple at Puri, Nagmahasaya declined their loving offer, saying: "The Master told me to remain at home. I cannot deviate one inch from his command."

Nagmahasaya fulfilled the law of the householder's life to the letter. His door was never closed, his self-sacrificing service never tired. Sometimes not only he fed those who came to him, but he met their travelling expenses as well. When one fell ill while in his house, he nursed him until he was quite recovered; then he hired a boat and sent him home, paying all the costs of the journey. What money he received from the rent of his small house in Calcutta rarely sufficed for this incessant output and often the family would be penniless for a time.

Once in the winter season two pious travellers asked shelter of him. The rain was falling heavily and the roof was in such disrepair that only one room of the four in his small house was dry. This he gave to his unexpected guests. "Come," he said to his wife, "we are fortunate indeed. Let us pass the night sitting on the porch and repeating the Lord's holy name."

It was impossible to have any repairs made so long as Nagmahasaya remained at home. Was a laborer called to mend a break in the roof thatch, Dr. Nag would prepare a *Chilum* (pipe of tobacco) for him, offer him food, and if still he persisted in working, he would sit beside him in the hot sun and fan him. If he went out on the river, he would make the boatmen rest while he plied the oars; and the men tried to avoid taking him, because it seemed to them a sin to let the saintly man labor while they sat idle. So completely did Nagmahasaya feel himself the servant of every human being, however lowly, that it was impossible for him to accept service from any one.

No *Sannyasin* (monk) could have led a more rigidly austere life than that which he marked out for himself. He covered his body with one coarse cotton cloth and walked barefooted in all seasons. He ate only the poorest food, without seasoning of any kind. Often he fasted days at a time and would say to friends who remonstrated with him: "If I am to think day and night of food only, when am I to think of God and do my devotional practices? Constant thought of food produces a kind of mania in man."

For four years he enjoyed the rare blessing of intimate association with Sri Ramakrishna, and during all that time he was the ideal disciple—unswerving in obedience, self-forgetting in devotion and zealously eager to render service. A last and precious opportunity came to him five days before the end. He had walked out from the city and was just entering the Master's room at Cossipore, when he overheard Sri Ramakrishna ask for an *Amalaki* fruit and a devotee reply that it could not be had, being out of season. Once before Nagmahasaya had arrived with an offering of oranges at the very moment when the Master expressed a desire to have one. He prayed the Divine Mother that She might bless him again and enable him to fulfill his Master's wish.

Without speaking to any one, he left the house and began a round of all the gardens in Calcutta. For two days no one saw him—he was searching for the fruit. On the third day he appeared before Sri Ramakrishna with an *Amalaki* in his hand. The Master's joy when he brought it was his parting benediction to him. Nagmahasaya never heard his voice again.

He was the embodiment of humility, chosen by the Master, it would seem, to teach the lesson of true lowliness to all his followers. Girish Chandra Ghose once said of him: "If a man is sincere and all idea of egotism has vanished from him, he attains the state of Nagmahasaya. The earth becomes consecrated by the very touch of the feet of such great men." And the disciple Narendra exclaimed one day: "Our life is passed vainly in the search after Truth; only he among us is the true son of our Master."

Mahendra Nath Gupta was also a faithful and humble householder son of Sri Ramakrishna. He has contributed a large share towards preserving the Master's teaching. Sri Ramakrishna never allowed any one to take notes when he talked. He would say: "Catch the spirit! If you are busy writing down what I say, you will get the letter, but you will lose the spirit." Mahendra Nath, however, was a professor and he could not resist the class-room habit of note-taking, so when the Master came to a pause in his teaching, he would slip out, hide behind a bush and write out what he could remember.

After Sri Ramakrishna had passed away, Mahendra was urged to publish these notes, but he found them too fragmentary. One day, however, he told me, when he had been reading some of them over, he began to meditate; in his meditation the scene where the notes were taken reconstituted itself and he heard the Master speak the words in full. This repeated itself day after day until he had a full record of his relation with the Master, both words and actions. The transcription of this he published in Bengali and in English under the title of "Gospel of Sri Ramakrishna."

When I knew Master Mahasaya, as Mahendra Nath was called by his associates, he was a tall impressive figure with white hair and long white beard; but when he first met Sri Ramakrishna in 1882, he was a young teacher of twenty-seven, holding the position of Head Master in the Vidyasagara High School at Calcutta. Sri Ramakrishna said of him to his nephew Ramlal: "This young man is a little older than the other boys, so he is somewhat grave. He remains serious and quiet when they are laughing and making merry." Mahendra's gravity was probably due to a feeling of awe. He was wonder-struck by the Master. One day it overwhelmed him and he exclaimed: "Never have I seen such marvellous wisdom, such love of God, such faith, renunciation, tolerance and universality in one person."

Mahendra came often to Dakshineswar and grew to be very dear to the Master, but the Master did not hesitate to rebuke him on occasion. Once at the Temple Mahendra Nath was discussing the subject of education with Narendra when Sri Ramakrishna joined them. He checked them abruptly with these words: "You can talk of worldly questions anywhere. When you come here, you must think and talk of God." Mere intellectual argument was always displeasing to Sri Ramakrishna. He demanded more fundamental thought and conversation from those who surrounded him.

Mahendra Nath told of a remarkable dream

he had which proved a turning point in his relation with the Master. He dreamed that the whole universe was a vast sheet of water. There were countless boats, but many sank in the flood. Only a few escaped. "I was on board a ship with a number of passengers," he said. "To our amazement we saw a Brahmin walking over the water. I cried out: 'How is it that you are walking on the water? Are you not afraid?' The Brahmin replied: 'There is nothing to fear. My feet rest on a bridge under the water.' I asked again: 'Where are you going?' 'To the city of the Mother,' the Brahmin responded. 'Wait a moment and I will come with you,' I called. 'I must hasten. It will take you too long. Mark the way I go. It will lead you to the Mother's city. Follow me!' the Brahmin gave answer." When Mahendra told this to the Master, the Master said: "A thrill runs through my body. The time has come for your initiation." So Mahendra became the disciple of Sri Ramakrishna.

Iswara Chandra Vidyasagara was one of the most eminent men of his time. His name declared him to be an "ocean of learning." His scholarship was extraordinary and his contribution to education not to be calculated. He established a Sanskrit College, he wrote and published a remarkable series of Sanskrit text books and collected a large library of rare volumes. As a philanthropist he was even greater than as a scholar. There was no measure or limit to his love for his fellow-man. It led him to serve him with boundless, tireless devotion. He gave his strength, his resources, his knowledge, his very life to the poor and down-trodden and the sorrowing, asking nothing in return. He was as much an ocean of compassion as he was an ocean of learning.

The meeting between Sri Ramakrishna and the *Pandit* in 1882 was a notable one:—the *Pandit* with his lofty intellectual vision, the Paramahamsa of Dakshineswar with his loftier spiritual vision; the one an "ocean of knowledge" and an equally vast ocean of love for humanity, the other a shoreless ocean of wisdom, compassion and tolerance. After they had greeted each other Sri Ramakrishna said to Vidyasagara: "Heretofore I have seen only canals, marshes and rivers, but to-day I have the good fortune to behold the ocean. You are a sea of *Vidya*—knowledge that leads Godward. You are not dry and hard as *Pandits* too often are. Your loving-kindness makes you soft and tender.

"So-called learned men talk of profound things but very few have any real knowledge of what they talk about. The highest learning is that by which we know God. Ordinary book-learning only confuses the mind. The knowledge leading Godward is the topmost step on the stairs by which one reaches the roof. The Absolute is the roof. Talking and controversy cease when true knowledge comes. The sign of true knowledge is the cessation of doubt and discussion. The one who has attained it is like a pitcher filled to the brim. When a pitcher is being filled, it gives out a gurgling sound; but when it is full all sound ceases. Reasoning and argument are uncertain guides."

Sri Ramakrishna spoke fervently of the Absolute and the Personal God; of Divine Mother, Her power and grace; of the world of Reality and the unreal world. Vidyasagara listened with grave deference to his words. Once he exclaimed: "I have learned something to-day!" When Sri Ramakrishna was leaving the *Pandit* said: "It will be my privilege and duty now to pay a visit to you." "A visit to me!" Sri Ramakrishna replied. "We are only small fishing boats which can row about in any water. You are a big merchant-ship. If you venture too far up stream, you may go aground on a sand-bank."

When Sri Ramakrishna arrived at Vidyasagara's house the *Pandit* had thought it sufficient to wait in the drawing-room to receive him. When the Master left, Vidyasagara himself accompanied him to the carriage door; and as the carriage drove away he stood looking after it with reverent gaze, his venerable figure lighted by the flickering candle in his hand.

COSSIPORE GARDEN

Sri Ramakrishna was no longer unknown. Throngs crowded the Temple enclosure every Sunday and throughout the week there was nearly always some one with him. Hour after hour he taught or counselled. Learned *Pandits* came to have their questions answered by this simple man who had no learning; wise *Sadhus* came to hear his words of wisdom; holy men came to pay homage to his superior holiness; men and women of every station came for instruction, help or comfort. He talked incessantly twenty hours out of the twenty-four and as a result he developed a serious affection of the throat.

Some have wondered how with his power he could have any malady at all. We are too often reluctant to accord to great souls human privileges. We expect them to sound a continuous superhuman note. If they did, they would miss the purpose of their coming to this earth. They take bodily form to expound humanity. Their life is the exposition of human life, a commentary and an example. They are here to solve humanity's problems. If they approach them from a different angle, with different conditions, they introduce new elements into their equations and create new problems, while mankind's problems remain unsolved.

The disciple Sasi once said that to him the greatest proof of Christ's divinity was the fact that he bore his crucifixion like a brave man. The power he used to raise Lazarus he might have used to free himself from the agony of the cross, but he did not do it. He saved others, himself he would not save. Why? Because he had come to teach men not to evade, but to endure; to suffer pain and persecution, yet forgive and trust. He knew that pain held a deeper lesson for the human heart than ease and he showed how that lesson could be learned. To have obliterated it or met it with superhuman power would have been to defeat its end.

Among those who surrounded Sri Ramakrishna were a few who were critical and carping. One gentleman asked him: "When you have so much power, why do you not heal yourself?" Sri Ramakrishna answered: "How can I turn this mind, which I have given wholly to God, back on this cage of flesh and bones?" The gentleman asked again: "Then why do you not beg your Divine Mother to heal you?" Sri Ramakrishna replied: "When I see my Divine Mother, I forget I have a body. How can I ask Her to heal it?"

There was another more palpable cause for the bodily disturbance that threatened the Master. An eminent physician of Calcutta, a critical materialist, defined it thus: "You allow people to touch your feet when you are in *Samadhi*. By doing this, you take on their troubles and that is the cause of your present malady." Sri Ramakrishna rejoined quickly: "That is why I do it. I wish to free them from their troubles."

When any one is in the superconscious state, he is highly sensitive and absorbs spontaneously the prevailing quality or condition of the one who touches him. In that state one needs to be protected from rude worldly contacts. That is the reason for the solitude of the mountain cave or the woodland glade. Sri Ramakrishna, however, had no desire to shield himself. When another person pleaded with him not to endanger his health, he exclaimed, "I would gladly give twenty thousand bodies to save one soul!"

This may sound chimerical to some ears. It is easy for the average mind to understand that if a man sees a tired woman in the street with a heavy load, he can take it and carry it for her. The load a world-weary soul carries is just as tangible and can be as successfully lifted. Vicarious atonement is a fact—not a specific fact, but a universal fact. We can all do more than bear one another's burdens, we can lift them. But to do this we must have no selfish burdens of our own. The hands must be free and the heart brave and loving.

Taking another's load means carrying it to its destination and accepting the weight and fatigue of it. The one who lifts the soul's burden must live out the *Karma* or condition which lies behind it. The debt must be paid to the last farthing, so the Bible says; or as the ancient Indo-Aryan law-giver, Manu, states it: "What a man sows, that must be reaped." Only a great soul, however, who has freed himself from the bondage of matter, can reap another's harvest of mistakes and pain. He alone can suffer for him; but the mind and heart of the great soul have transcended the plane of *Karma* or material suffering, so the body is the only place where he can live out another's troubles. Thus it was that Sri Ramakrishna's body was attacked. He took upon himself burden after burden until the body broke under the accumulated weight; and as the throat was the part most severely taxed, it gave way at that point.

Waning strength warned devotees and disciples that the Master needed more watchful care than he could receive at the Temple, so it was decided to take him to Calcutta. A house was procured in the Baghbazar district, but it was found undesirable and he went to Balaram's home. At the end of a week, however, it was apparent that there was little hope of quiet there. Crowds sought him out as persistently as at Dakshineswar and he talked as continuously; so another house was hired at Shyampukur, also a district of Calcutta. This was in September, 1885. In December for fresher air and yet greater quiet he was moved to Cossipore, an outlying quarter of the city.

Later when I visited the Cossipore house it was the monsoon season and a light rain was falling, casting a shadow of greyness over everything; but if the sun had been shining, I imagine there would have been the same twilight dimness, so dense was the tropical growth which filled the garden. A very high wall surrounded it, giving a sense of seclusion and solitude. Passing through a tall gateway, we went up a tree-shaded driveway of some length to the house. On the way, to the right, was a large pool with cement edge and nearer the house, on the left, was a second smaller pool.

At some seventy-five feet from the gate the driveway curved and ran parallel with the front garden wall, throwing the side of the house towards the street, with the smaller pool, thick clumps of shrubbery and the high wall between. The inner end of the driveway formed a loop passing under a porte-cochere, with roof terrace above. Behind this was a large room which Sri Ramakrishna had occupied while there. It was on this upper terrace that he had spent a whole morning, writing or drawing invisible signs with his finger on the brick floor. His attention was so fixed, his thought so abstracted, that no one dared approach or ask him what he was doing, but undoubtedly he was solving some profound problem of life. No one ever learned what it was and Sri Ramakrishna himself never referred to it.

In this lovely garden and large house the Master spent the closing days of his life. The disciple Sasi in telling me of them gave this picture: "There came the question who was to take care of Sri Gurumaharaj. We were at that time all studying in the Colleges. Narendra was just preparing to pass his B. L. degree; I, my B. A.; and Sarat, I believe, his F. A. But we could not fix our minds on our books, so we gave up attending the classes and devoted all our time to attending on the Master.

"With so many of us there, it became necessary to hire a cook, and we got a man from his village. He was a Brahmin but such a rustic that he could not even sit cross-legged without great difficulty. He was used to working all day in his fields and when he sat, he squatted on his legs. His cooking was so bad that we all began to go down under it. Then Holy Mother begged so hard to come and cook for Gurumaharaj that he said she might come.

"One day, however, for some reason she was not there, so the cook carried Gurumaharaj's food to him. With great difficulty he got up the stairs, so lumbering and awkward was he; and when he had placed the food before Gurumaharaj, he wanted to run away. But Gurumaharaj called him back and told him to sit down. Although he was such a rustic, he was simple; there was absolutely no crookedness in him. Gurumaharaj merely reached over and touched him and at once the man went into *Samadhi.* He stayed in that state for fully two hours. When he came back to his senses and opened his eyes, they were fiery red and he asked me: 'Where am I?' He could not walk and Gurumaharaj asked me to lead him away. As I did so, I asked him what he had been experiencing. 'Oh! I was not here,' he replied. 'All this while I have been worshipping my Divine Mother.' "

Holy Mother told me: "It was really through this cook that I got my photograph of Thakur (Sri Ramakrishna). A photographer had taken some pictures of Thakur when he was in *Samadhi* and knew nothing of it. One Sunday the first photographs were brought to Cossipore Garden by the photographer, and at once they were all taken by the *Bhaktas* (devotees), except this one which every one thought was too dark. The cook begged it from Gurumaharaj, who gave it to him; but as he was going back to his village for a time, he asked me to keep it for him until he should claim it. He never returned to ask me for it, so I have had it ever since and while all the other pictures of the same period are faded and grey, mine is as fresh and clear as if it had been taken only yesterday."

When the pictures were brought to Sri Ramakrishna, he showed the keenest interest in them. He took one and stood it up against the bolster on the bed, looked at it again and again and made many comments on it, but his manner and words were as impersonal as if it was the picture of an utter stranger.

Navagopal's wife related to me another significant incident in connection with this picture. "Once I went to Cossipore Garden," she said, "but I found so many visitors there that I could not go upstairs. I waited for some time and then Gurumaharaj sent down one of his photographs saying: 'Tell her to be content with looking at this to-day.' Later he told me, in referring to the picture, that it 'would travel in railway carriages and on ocean steamers and by bearers; and people would carry it in their pockets and even on their watch chains.' "

This seems a prophecy in the light of what has happened since. In Prague a Bohemian artist painted a large portrait of Sri Ramakrishna some years ago. His sister had given him a copy of the "Gospel" by Mahendra and it had so fired his heart that he wrote for all the photographs he could procure and made the portrait. When the disciple Rakhal saw the first small sketch of it which the artist had sent to me, his comment was: "It is not a perfect likeness, but he has caught the spirit."

In France and Switzerland, Italy, Germany, Holland, Sweden, Denmark and Norway, in England and Russia there are houses where a picture of Sri Ramakrishna stands in reverent apartness. It has found its way to Canada and to every part of the United States. It has gone around the world with more than one devout traveller and it is appearing with growing frequency in Western books on India.

Thus life went on in the deep-shadowed garden at Cossipore, the younger men serving with fervent self-forgetting devotion, the older householders bearing the financial burden of the large establishment. The younger ones offered to take even that and meet the cost of their living by begging, like real mendicant monks. One day they did go out with begging bags, bring home food and cook it, much to the Master's delight. It gave him joy to see them independent and of courageous spirit, but the householder disciples were wounded by this show of independence and begged their share in providing for the Master. Everything was adjusted and after that the days passed peacefully in that upper room with its exalted atmosphere of holy quietude.

Narendra, Rakhal, Latu, Sasi, Sarat and Gopaldada lived at Cossipore with the Master; other disciples came and went. By degrees each was given special duties. Holy Mother prepared the Master's meals and carried them to him. Sri Ramakrishna's niece Lakshmi or Lakididi, as she was called, helped her in the kitchen. Sometimes other women disciples came to be with Holy Mother for a few days and share in the service of the Master. Two of the boys went to the bazar and did the marketing. The other boys watched beside the Master and attended to his needs. The disciple Sasi told me that they took turns, each one remaining six hours at a time.

One night near the close, the disciple Sasi was watching. There was a chill in the air. Sri Ramakrishna rose from his bed. Sasi who was sitting by his door came in quickly and began to scold; but Sri Ramakrishna reached feebly for his dressing gown and gave it to Sasi, saying: "I want you to have it." Sasi took it reluctantly; then not feeling that he was worthy to keep it, gave it to Rakhal, who lost it while on pilgrimage. This little incident shows how lovingly the Master watched over those who watched over him.

THE PASSING

The Master's body was breaking. It could take no more burdens. It could bear no more weight. The spirit, however, remained undaunted and tireless. To give was his life. It hurt him to have the disciples deny access to his devotees. They did it to shield him and safeguard his strength, but it hurt him none the less. One day a gentleman came to see him. It was the one who as a youth had thought to give him a good lesson. He had dressed himself as a *Zemindar* in great elegance that he might gain surer admission, but he was not allowed to enter. No word of it was carried to the Master, but suddenly Sri Ramakrishna began to weep, saying: "Why do you keep my devotee from me? I must see him." Then he was told of the visitor.

"When he heard who it was, he had him brought in at once," the disciple Sasi related. "I was in the room at the time, but Gurumaharaj sent me out and the two were alone for a long while. Then the Master called me back and told me to bring one of his photographs. This he took and with his own hand gave it to the gentleman. The gentleman took it and without speaking a word to any one, ran out of the house as if he was mad. From that moment he lost all consciousness of the world, of everything, and day and night he sat repeating *'Priya Nath, Priya Nath'* (Blessed Lord,

Blessed Lord). When all the rest of the community was sleeping, one could hear those words sounding out in the silence of the night. He did not even remember to eat unless his wife put food into his mouth.

"He never returned to Gurumaharaj. Like the pearl oyster he had got the drop of *Swati* rain and needed nothing more. But after Gurumaharaj passed away, he used to come often to our *Math* (monastery) at Baranagore. For several months he came every evening. He would go straight to the Shrine, sit and meditate there for some time, then go away without even coming to the part of the house where we lived. Sometimes he would sing and he had a very beautiful voice. There was one song of which Sri Ramakrishna was particularly fond and he would sing it again and again. In this way would our Master transform a life."

The wife of Navagopal once carried some sweetmeats to Sri Ramakrishna at Cossipore. She told me of it thus: "As I stood hesitatingly before him, he asked: 'What do you want?' 'I want to give you some sweetmeats,' I said. 'Very well!' and he let me put some in his mouth. Still I stood before him. 'Are you satisfied?' he asked. 'No? Then what do you want?' I clasped my hands and answered: 'I want to give you more sweetmeats.' He let me put a little more in his mouth, and seeing me still unsatisfied, he asked the question a third time. When again I asked to feed him, he said: 'No; no more now. Wait. In my *Sukshma Sarira* (subtle body) I shall take all the sweetmeats you and everyone can offer me.' "

The Master poured out blessings on his disciples with unstinted bounty. To some he gave the gift of illumination, to others the promise of it. On one householder he bestowed the power to see the living Presence in every sacred image. With Narendra and Rakhal he was particularly tender. He fondled them as a mother might fondle a little one in arms. "While we were living with Gurumaharaj at the Cossipore Garden house," the disciple Sasi said to me, "there was a period when Naren spent all his time in meditation or in making *Japam* (repeating the Lord's name) until his eyes were red and he did not even come to serve Gurumaharaj.

"His longing to realize God was so intense that he declared: 'If by taking a handful of filth and swallowing it, I could realize God, I would do it.' One evening when I went to call him to his meal, he was sitting in meditation; and just as an expression of affection I ran my hand over his back. It was at once stained with blood. I looked and saw that his whole back was covered with mosquitoes and was bleeding. He was completely unconscious of it."

From Yogin-ma I heard: "The night on which Naren took *Mantram* (received initiation) from

Thakur he was like a madman. It was at Cossipore Garden and all night he walked excitedly round and round the house. Finally he went to Thakur and said, 'Give me peace.' Thakur said to him: 'How little you can bear! This fire that is lighted in your heart I bore in mine for twelve years and you cannot bear it for one night, but come crying for peace. What do you want?' Naren said: 'Give me *Nirvikalpa Samadhi*' (the highest superconscious state). Thakur replied: 'You are already beyond that. That is a very little thing for you to ask for,' but he touched his heart and put him in the state of *Samadhi*. Afterwards he said to him: 'The key is with me. You have a certain work for me to do in the world. When that is done and you come to know who you are, you will not stay here.'

"At another time when the disciples had been meditating in Sri Ramakrishna's room, Naren happened to be sitting next to a boy who was very eager to realize, but who was little advanced spiritually. As Naren came out from his meditation, he leaned over and touched the boy. Thakur rebuked him saying: 'The power you have is not yours to give away. It is given you for a special purpose to be used later.' "

On Narendra Sri Ramakrishna bestowed the chief power; but to Rakhal, Baburam, Sasi, Sarat, to Kali, Tarak, Gangadhar, to each beloved disciple he transmitted some special gift. He kept nothing for himself. Now his earthly mission was done. He asked a devotee to read to him the almanac and he chose an auspicious moment, as if preparing for a journey, but he spoke no word of what that journey was. The disciples knew only too well. The toll of the passing bell was sounding silently in their ears, but they refused to heed it. The time had come. The Master was going. The sun was setting.

Let the story of the last hours in that upper room be told by the disciple Sasi who lived through them:—

"We all thought the Master was better because he ate so much more supper than usual, and he said nothing of going. In the afternoon he had asked Yogin to look in the almanac and see whether it was an auspicious day. Also he had been telling us for some time that the vessel which was floating in the ocean was already two-thirds full of water, soon the rest would fill up and it would plunge into the ocean. But we did not believe that he was really going. He never seemed to mind the pain. He never lost his cheerfulness. He used to say that he was all well and happy, only there was a little something here (pointing to the throat). 'Within me are two persons,' he would declare. 'One is the Divine Mother, the other is her devotee. It is the devotee that has been taken ill.'

"When Sri Ramakrishna gave up his body I think it was the most blissful moment of his life.

A thrill of joy ran through him. I myself saw it. I remember every incident of that last day. Our Master seemed very well and cheerful. In the afternoon he talked for fully two hours to a gentleman who had come to put him some questions about Yoga. A little later I ran some seven miles to bring the doctor. When I reached the doctor's house, he was not there; but I was told that he was at a certain place, so I ran another mile and met him on the way. He had an engagement and said he could not come, but I dragged him away just the same.

"On that last night Ramakrishna was talking with us to the very last. For supper he had drunk a whole half glass of *Payasam* (gruel) and seemed to relish it. There was no doubt a little heat in the body, so he asked us to fan him and some ten of us were all fanning at once. He was sitting up against five or six pillows which were supported by my body and at the same time I too was fanning. This made a slight motion and twice he asked me: 'Why are you shaking?' It was as if his mind was so fixed and steady that he could perceive the least motion. Narendra took his feet and began to rub them and Ramakrishna was talking to him, telling what he must do. 'Take care of these boys,' he repeated again and again, as if he was putting them in Naren's charge. Then he asked to lie down.

"Suddenly at one o'clock he fell towards one side, there was a low sound in the throat and I saw all the hairs of his body stand on end. Narendra quickly laid his feet on a quilt and ran downstairs as if he could not bear it. A doctor, who was a great devotee and who was feeling his pulse, saw that it had stopped and began to weep aloud. 'What are you doing?' I asked, impatient with him for acting as if the Master had really left us.

"We all believed that it was only *Samadhi*, so Naren came back and we sat down, some twenty of us, and began repeating all together: 'Hari Om! Hari Om!' In this way we waited until between one and two the next day. Still the body had some heat in it, especially about the back, but the doctor insisted that the soul had left it. About five the body had grown cold, so we placed it on a cot, covered with garlands and carried it to the burning-ghat."

A large horizontal tablet on a high rectangular base now marks the spot beside the Ganges where Sri Ramakrishna's body was cremated. Near by stands a tall bush covered with scarlet blossoms—those that the Master used daily at the Temple in the worship of the Divine Mother—and at the foot of a broad flight of steps the river flows by in swift-rushing current.

The memory of the Master's presence pervades the Temple, the burning-ghat, the green-veiled garden at Cossipore, the upper room in Balaram's house, even the surging river seems to tell of him.

He is not absent from any place or life that he touched while in the flesh. When at the appointed time, Holy Mother was removing her bracelets and exchanging her wifely *Sari* for the plain white unbordered cloth of the widow, it is said that Sri Ramakrishna appeared before her and asked reproachfully: "What are you doing? I have not gone away." In penitent salutation Holy Mother clasped her hands and bowed her head, then silently she put back her bangles and her bordered *Sari*.

REACH OF THE MESSAGE

A humble priest, without learning, who never went out to preach, made no far journeys, never sought a following or proclaimed himself, yet to-day his message reaches round the world! It has been heard on the steppes of Siberia and in the hills of Tuscany; on the banks of the Rhine and beside the fjords of Norway; in Argentina, Canada and Japan, in England and France and America, in China and over the whole of India. It has been translated into English, Spanish, French, German, Swedish and Persian, as well as into numerous Indian vernaculars; while the life-story of the one who gave the message has lain on American news-stands, English book-stalls, and German book-shelves; and at the present moment a prominent French writer is preparing a French version of it.

Who carried this pervasive message? Not Sri Ramakrishna. He said often that his body was unfitted to the rude work of the pioneer. It was too highly sensitized. It was made to receive the message, not to give it to the greater world. He conveyed it to those immediately about him and left it to them to transmit it to the wider circle. Especially on the disciple Narendra was laid the task of carrying it to humanity at large. The Congress of Religions at Chicago provided a first and priceless opportunity for presenting it. How he went there was told me by the one who did most towards making that going possible,—a professor in a leading college of Madras. I shall repeat it just as he spoke it, with its touches of humor and its graver touches.

"It was in December, 1892, that a friend came to Madras from Mysore and told of a northern *Sadhu* who had made a deep impression upon every one at Pondicherry (French India), where he had been stopping for a time. Then a second one came from Pondicherry with the same story; so when the *Sannyasin* arrived in Madras several of us went to see him. We had two conversations with him and then we began going to him every day.

"On the second day, I remember, he talked of the East and the West and he said: 'You (the Hindus) need more ruggedness and the West needs more gentleness.' I asked: 'Why do you not go to the Parliament of Religions at Chicago to represent Hinduism?' 'I have no objection to going,' he replied, 'if some one will send me.' One of us offered him some money (two Rupees). It was the first time he had taken money and he laughed and said: 'I will give it to the first beggar I meet;' and actually he gave it to some poor beggar. When the first subscription for his journey came (two hundred and fifty Rupees) he took it, went at once to the shops and bought a cart and a number of toys for some children whom he loved very much.

"He sailed in the fourth week of June from Bombay. While we were at Bombay together, we said to him: 'Swami, you are going to America; time is very precious there. You must have a watch.' 'All right; buy me one,' was his quick answer. 'You should also have some visiting cards.' 'Very well, have one hundred printed.' At that time he was known as Satchidananda—but when I asked: 'What name am I to put on the cards, he replied: 'Swami Vivekananda.' It was the first time that he used that name.

"He had his European clothes stitched at Bombay. When they were brought home he dressed himself in them and looked very grand. Then we drove to Cook's to get the circular notes, afterward to buy the new watch. This was Swamiji's first experience of circular notes and of a Gladstone bag. The trousers of the new suit he had bought were a little long and were getting dirty. I had some one call his attention to it several times. Finally he said: 'Why do you keep reminding me of my trousers? They will take us for a set of barbarians. Don't you know that I am perfectly accustomed to this dress?'

"After he reached Chicago, he wrote that it was a very costly place and he was not going to stay for the Parliament. He cabled from Boston for money to come home. I had none, so I wired to the Maharajah of Khetri, who sent him by cable about one thousand Rupees. Later we collected and sent seven hundred Rupees. Before it reached him, he wrote that we need not bother any more about money, as he had spoken at the Parliament with great success and now everyone was ready to do for him there."

Narendra did not accept his task eagerly. When Sri Ramakrishna laid it in his hand, he said: "No, No; I do not wish to be bound." "But it was for this I brought you here," Sri Ramakrishna insisted. Still Narendra demurred, but finally his opposition was overcome. As he sat on the platform at the Parliament of Religions facing that vast concourse of people there was the same unwillingness in his heart and again and again he begged the presiding officer to delay his turn. He shrank from his public errand. At last he was announced. He rose and silently repeating a Sanskrit prayer in which occurs the line "Thou canst make the dumb to speak eloquently," he began his address. At its close the great audience stood up and cheered.

He had delivered his Master's message and it had been heard. What lent to his words such impelling force? The voice of the Brahmin of Dakshineswar sounded through them. The eloquence of vision was in them.

Sri Ramakrishna's message continues to spread. It is a significant sign that in the Master's village home in India a room has been set apart for foreign pilgrims. At the head monastery of the large religious community which has grown out of his life there are also special quarters for foreign guests; provision is made for receiving them at all the Centres connected with the Master's work. These Centres, bearing Sri Ramakrishna's name and resting on his teaching, are innumerable in India. There are even some in the Occident, which do not bear his name but which draw inspiration from his life.

What is the secret of this simple Brahmin's message? Why has it gone forth so quickly? Because it meets a fundamental need. It brings to a discord-stricken world the word of unity, tolerance, universal brotherliness; oneness of Deity and oneness of humanity. The message is not a new one. Novelty exists only in little things. The great messages of the world are glorified by their sameness. Truth is one and as man approaches it, unity overshadows variety in the measure of values.

A spiritual message, if true, will never be new. It cannot be new. A great soul comes and proclaims it; it starts on its way, loses momentum, fades out of man's daily practice and needs a new voice and a new life to proclaim it once more. Sri Ramakrishna spoke the word and lived the life and gave the message. It rests with mankind to hear it.

TEACHINGS

In Sri Ramakrishna's teachings there are no stereotyped doctrines or dogmas, no rigid church canons. There is no creed to repeat, no catechism to learn. He does not insist even on Scriptural study. Upon one thing alone does he lay uncompromising stress—on living, embodying the faith in the life, being what one believes. To put it in his own homely phrase: "Mind and mouth must be one;" that is, thought and life must coincide. One must be genuine all the way through.

Unswerving fidelity to the Ideal he places at the foundation of all moral and spiritual growth; but according to him merit or growth rests less on the form of the Ideal than on the degree of the fidelity. It matters less, he claims, what a man worships than in what spirit he worships. The very act of worship will enlarge the outlook and by an inevitable reaction the Ideal will assume a new and higher form. "If a person is sincere and yearns towards God," are his words, "he will in the end realize Him, whether he knows philosophy or not. If in his search after the Lord he takes a wrong path the Lord will lead him forth to the goal, provided he thirsts after Him.

"There was a time when in mad yearning I would throw myself on the ground under the *Panchavati* and cry aloud to my Divine Mother for more light, saying: 'Grant unto me that I may realize God in all aspects.' Many think that knowledge of God cannot be attained without the study of books; but higher than reading is hearing, higher than hearing is seeing. Better than reading about Benares is hearing directly of it from one who has been there; better than hearing of it, is seeing it with one's own eyes.

"Too often people depend on outer authority rather than on direct sight. A gentleman once said to his friend: 'Yesterday as I was passing along the street, Mukerji's house collapsed with a terrible crash.' 'Let me see if there is anything about it in the newspaper,' the friend replied. He found nothing and said it could not be true. 'But I saw it with my own eyes,' the gentleman insisted. 'You must be mistaken,' the friend retorted, 'there is nothing about it in the paper.' "

God was a palpable fact to Sri Ramakrishna. He had gazed upon Deity in its personal aspect. He had also visioned the Absolute. Those three days and nights of supreme contemplation in that locked chamber after taking his final vows had lifted him to the plane of pure being where he had beheld unclothed Divinity. Now with unwavering conviction he exhorted man not to accept invisibility as a proof of non-existence, but to recognize that it was his own blindness that veiled the face of God. "You see many stars at night in the sky," he exclaimed, "but find them not when the sun rises; can you say that there are no stars in the heaven of day? So, O man! because you behold not God in the days of your ignorance, say not there is no God."

Seeing God leads the thought automatically to a recognition of His oneness, Sri Ramakrishna maintained. Infinity cannot be multiplied. There cannot be more than one Infinite Being. Deity with form and formless, personal and impersonal, manifested and unmanifested—all must be contained in that Being. Sri Ramakrishna illustrated this by a parable:—

"Two persons were hotly disputing as to the color of a chameleon. One said, 'The chameleon on that palm tree is of a beautiful red color.' The other replied, 'You are mistaken, the chameleon is not red, but blue.' Not being able to settle the matter by argument, both went to the person who lived under that tree and had watched the chameleon in all its phases of color. One of them said: 'Sir, is not the chameleon on that tree a red color?' The person replied, 'Yes, sir.' The other disputant said: 'What do you say? It is not red, it is blue.' The person again replied quietly: 'Yes, it is blue.' He knew that the chameleon constantly changes color; thus it was that he said 'Yes' to both of these conflicting statements.

"The Supreme likewise has many forms. The devotee who has seen God in one aspect only, knows Him in that aspect alone. But only he who has seen Him in manifold aspects is in a position to say, 'All these forms are of one God and God is multiform.' He is formless and with form, and many are His forms which no one knows.

"Fire itself has no definite shape, but in glowing embers it assumes certain forms. The formless fire is then endowed with form. Similarly the formless God sometimes invests Himself with definite form. As water when congealed becomes ice, so the visible form of the Almighty is the condensed manifestation of the all-pervading formless Brahman. It may be called, in fact, the Absolute solidified. As ice is part and parcel of the water, remains in the water and afterwards melts into it, so the Personal God is part and parcel of the Impersonal. He rises from the Impersonal, remains there, and ultimately merges into it."

According to Sri Ramakrishna ignorance is the consciousness of many things, seeing variety. True knowledge is the consciousness of unity, knowledge of oneness. Beholding God "face to face" is realization. Unity and variety both vanish when realization comes. "Suppose you get a thorn in your foot," he would say; "you take another thorn to get it out. When the thorn is out, you throw both away."

" 'I' and 'mine' make up ignorance. 'Thou' and 'Thine' make up knowledge. The true devotee saith: 'Lord, Thou art the only Doer. I am an instrument in Thy hands. I act as I am made to act by Thee. Thine are all these riches, this house, this family, everything. Nothing is mine. I am only a servant. Mine is only to serve according to Thy bidding.' "

Out of the sense of oneness grows inevitably the spirit of universal tolerance and brotherliness which forms the background of all Sri Ramakrishna's thought. Intolerance springs from a sense of difference, and this sense of difference comes from superficiality. All differences lie on the surface. As we approach the depths and heights of being, we advance nearer and nearer to a central unit. Differences vanish. Sri Ramakrishna describes it thus: "When a man is on the plain he sees the lowly grass and the lofty tree; but when he ascends to the mountain top, tall trees and lowly grass all become one indistinguishable mass of verdure."

This does not mean that Sri Ramakrishna wished to level everything down to a homogeneous flatness. "Diversity is the essential law of creation," he declares, but he adds that beneath this diversity is an equally essential unity; and only as we learn to place our accent on that, shall we heal the wounds of the world, inflicted by warring intolerance and discord. If God is one, all mankind becomes one and clash of interests is effaced.

What is Sri Ramakrishna's attitude towards this outer diversified world? It can be defined most aptly in words which Ernest Renan wrote when speaking of St. Francis of Assisi and himself. "Like the patriarch of Assisi," says Renan, "I have travelled through the world without being attached to it, a humble lodger, if I may put it that way. Both of us, while possessing nothing of our own, have yet felt ourselves rich. God gave us the temporary use of the world and we have been content to enjoy without possessing."

Sri Ramakrishna's words are: "To lead the life of a householder is not wrong, but take care that you live and work without attachment, with your mind always fixed on God. . . . Do your work in the world with one hand and hold the Feet of the Lord with the other. When your work is done, fold the Feet of the Lord to your heart with both your hands."

Although Sri Ramakrishna was lenient and tolerant towards the world and its enjoyments, he grew stern and reproachful when he dealt with worldliness. "The boat may be in the water, but the water must not be in the boat; so man may be in the world, but the world must not be in him," he would say. And again: "So long as a piece of iron is in the furnace, it is red hot, but it grows black very soon when it is taken out. So also is it with the worldly man. So long as he is in church or with pious people, he is full of religious feeling, but as soon as he leaves the church and his pious associations, his worldly interests seize upon him again."

"Worldly men repeat the name of the Lord and perform good deeds, but they do it for reward and when misfortune comes they forget all about the Divine name—like a parrot who will repeat a holy word by rote, but when a cat comes it goes back to its cry of 'Kaw, Kaw.' "

"The man immersed in worldliness cannot see God. Does the muddy water reflect the sun? As the troubled surface of rolling water gives only a broken image of the sun, so the mind that is disturbed by worldly desires and passions cannot fully reflect the light of God."

To a world-worn elderly man, who came to him for counsel and refreshment, he said sadly: "You sought the world first and now you seek God. If you had sought God first and the world after, how different would have been your life!" He exclaimed at another time: "He who is a thief of his own thoughts does not accomplish anything. If you say that God is your all-in-all while your mind makes the world its all-in-all, what benefit can you derive? How can you hope to see God if your whole heart and soul do not long for Him?"

Sri Ramakrishna was often asked, what keeps a man from seeing God? His answer was: "Egoism is the cloud that hides the Lord from our sight. When egoism vanishes, God is seen in His full glory. If I hold up this cloth before me, you will no longer see me; yet I shall be just as near you. So God is nearer to you than anything; yet because of the screen of egotism, you cannot see Him."

The disciple Sasi remarked to me one day: "Sri Ramakrishna never taught a vague religion, he never spoke in vague terms." This definiteness so characteristic of him, makes his teaching sound at times brusque and unbending; but with all his arraignment of worldliness and insincerity, there was never any one more tender and forgiving towards blundering mankind than he. He used to say that there was no greater sin than to call a man a sinner. He could not bear the word "sin," and once he had the Bible carried from the room because in reading it, he chanced to open to a passage containing a prophetic outburst against the evil ways of sinners.

He exhorted men not to dwell on their limitations and failures. "Do not waste your time on repentance. That is a foolish idea," he would say. He believed in a saner, more constructive method of correcting humanity's faults and mistakes. He roused the latent perfection in the soul. He reminded a man of his true nature, but he did not try to make him perfect all at once, he knew that would break the body. A perfect nature, to manifest, must have a perfectly adapted body.

He believed perfection was best attained by waking a man's own spirit; then even if he is overpowered again, that spirit within will force him to keep on struggling until perfection is reached. "Many times must a man sink and struggle in water," he said, "before he learns to swim. So none can enjoy at once the felicity of swimming calmly on the ocean of Divine bliss until he has made himself fit for it by wearisome struggles and trials."

Sri Ramakrishna followed every soul born of woman through these trials and struggles with pulsing sympathy. He strove in its striving, he suffered in its pain; yet he did not offer sedative remedies. He sought less to ease the pain, to minimize the struggle, than to lift the soul above them. He tried to make the heart heroic and brave and persevering.

He did this by applying various methods. Sometimes he carried the seeker along the path of activity, sometimes he enjoined meditation. Sometimes he taught monism, sometimes dualism; but always was he unvarying in advocating the practice of devotion as the best cure for the ills of the present time. "Men in this age will do better to follow the path of devotion. Let them love, pray and surrender themselves to the Lord." He believed that only by this simple natural means would they counteract the unrest and conflict and materialism that rend and weight the earth today.

But whatever the remedy he counselled, whatever the method he adopted, one appeal only was on his lips. It was this and it seems to sum up all his teaching: "Go forward, my children, and never lose sight of your Ideal. Move onward and stop not until you have reached the goal. Having reached one stage of your journey, do not imagine you have come to your journey's end. March on and never halt until you have attained the great Ideal of your life—seeing God!"

CHARACTER

There is no more difficult task than to try to portray the character of a great soul. Character is defined most often by enumeration of details, the listing of human traits. But the nature of the great soul has in it none of the petty details characteristic of ordinary men. It has a bigger, wider sweep. It can be depicted only as the Japanese draw their sacred mountain Fujiyama—a thin outline of a towering height and within it a glowing white surface, devoid of small lines and shadows. With the great soul the thin enclosing line is the human, the broad expanse of shining whiteness is the divine.

So was it with the character of Sri Ramakrishna. The disciple Sasi said of him: "In Ramakrishna there was absolutely no ego left. He could not use the first personal pronoun 'I.' He would say: 'Why do you not come here?' (meaning to him) 'Mother will illumine you.' In him the divine was fully manifested. He preached God, nothing but God, and his whole nature was God-like. We never knew what purity was, we never knew what perfection was, what God was, until we saw him.

"He knew everything. Did any one go to him with a morose or sorrowful heart? At once he would feel it in his own heart and would give peace. Everything he did was for others. He was not necessitated to come to this world, but he came to help mankind; and every movement of his body, every movement of his mind was directed towards the amelioration of his fellow-men.

"Ramakrishna was able to supply to every man just what he needed. Sometimes a man would come from a distant place with his heart panting for God, but seeing the room full of people, he would shrink back and hide himself in a dim corner. Without a word Ramakrishna would walk to him and touch him and in a moment he was illumined.

"By that touch, Ramakrishna really swallowed ninety-nine per cent of the man's *Karma* (results of actions). Taking others' *Karma* was the reason he had his last long illness. He used to tell us: 'The people whose *Karma* I have taken think that they are attaining salvation through their own strength. They do not understand that it is because I have taken their *Karma* on me.' We do not know how much we owe to him; but some day we shall realize what he has done for us and then we shall know how to be grateful to him.

"The only real enemy Sri Ramakrishna ever had was a man who was very jealous of the devotion of Mathura Babu for him. He insisted that Ramakrishna must have exercised some special powers to captivate such a rich man. The man determined to find out what Gurumaharaj had done, so one day when Ramakrishna was alone, he came to the Temple and asked him. 'I have done nothing,' Gurumaharaj replied. 'What could I do?' The man, believing that he was only deceiving him, placed the heel of his boot on Gurumaharaj's toe and began to press it, saying: 'Tell me. You must tell me what powers you have used.' Like an abused child, Gurumaharaj insisted: 'I do not know what you mean. I have done nothing.' The man went away angry. Ramakrishna said nothing about it; but later for some unknown reason the family of this man was completely ruined.

"Ramakrishna was the embodiment of truthfulness. He always said: 'No man can hope to realize the Truth who is not absolutely truthful.' Once he had been invited by a certain gentleman to assist at a religious discussion. When the day came, it was pouring rain. With great difficulty we procured a carriage two miles away from Dakshineswar and because of the heavy down-pour the coachman asked three times the usual price; but Gurumaharaj said: 'I have given my word, so I must go.' He got in the carriage, drove four or five miles and when he reached the house, he found the gate bolted on the inside. He knocked but no one came, so he repeated three times to the gate: 'I have come, I have come, I have come.' Then he got into the carriage again and drove back to Dakshineswar, perfectly satisfied because he had kept his word.

"Sri Ramakrishna practised the most perfect simplicity in his habits. Once some one brought him a silver tongue-scraper; he refused to take it and sent me to buy a most ordinary brass one for a quarter of an Anna. He showed that the simpler is the man, the happier he is. His spirit of renunciation was without reservation or compromise. One day he saw an especially fine mango and he had a mind to take it, but he could not raise his hand to pluck it. Another day he tried to pick a fruit, but with the same result. He was unable to lift his arm; the muscles refused to obey him. 'You see,' he explained, 'a *Sannyasin* should never store anything, so the Divine Mother will not let me lay by this fruit even for a few hours.'"

Childlike obedience to his Divine Mother lay at the very root of his character. It was the impelling factor in all his action. Devotion for Her gave form to his thought and direction to his will. From it sprang his every impulse, his every desire. His daily prayer was:

"O Mother Divine! I throw myself upon Thy mercy. May the Lotus of Thy Feet keep me from whatever leadeth Thy children away from Thee! I seek not, Good Mother, the pleasures of the senses. I seek not fame. Nor do I long for those powers which enable one to perform miracles. What I pray for, O Mother, is pure love for Thee, love untainted by desires, love without alloy, love that seeketh not the things of the world, love that welleth up unbidden from the depths of the immortal soul!

"Grant likewise, Mother, that Thy child, bewitched by the allurements of this deluding world, may not forget Thee—yes, forget Thee, entangled in the net of lust and greed, which Thou in *Maya's* form has woven round me. Grant that I may never be charmed into loving these!

"Mother Divine, seest Thou not that Thy child has none else in all the world beside Thee? Alas! I know not how to chant Thy name! Devoid am I of deep devotion for Thee, of knowledge too that leadeth to Thee; devoid of genuine love for Thee. Vouchsafe unto me that love, O Mother, out of Thine infinite and unfailing mercy!"

We must not imagine that Sri Ramakrishna had no points of spontaneous contact with humanity. He touched it at many points. His natural sense of humor provided one happy meeting-ground. With it he broke down many barriers and swept aside carping criticism. To a doctor in the course of a conversation on medical causes and remedies he remarked with a twitch of the lips: "A man once said to his physician, 'My coach drove under a tamarind tree covered with sour fruit and I have got acidity of the stomach.' The doctor, no less ready of wit, answered: 'The captain of a ship once had a headache. The doctors on board held a consultation and had a blister applied to the side of the ship. Once I was called to see a child with whooping-cough and I tried to find out how it had caught the disease. At last I discovered that the ass which supplied the milk for the child had got drenched with the rain.' Sri Ramakrishna and the doctor both laughed heartily.

Girish Ghose once told me that he thought to shock Sri Ramakrishna by singing a verse from an indecent song. It was in the early rebellious days of their association. Sri Ramakrishna smiled and with twinkling eyes sang an equally lawless verse. At once, Girish Babu said, he felt like a silly boy trying to be funny. This manner of meeting attack was characteristic of Sri Ramakrishna. His method was most often homeopathic. He cured like by like. He did not condemn a man's evil ways. He made him feel how foolish and unprofitable they were; and he tried, if he could, to laugh him out of them. Laughter was a more acceptable weapon to his hand than rebuke.

Another effective point of contact with the human was his gift of song. Many a heart was stirred and reclaimed, many a pain or distress was soothed by his singing. Sometimes his teaching would be given wholly in melody. He would sing song after song with exuberant devotion and delight. He possessed a rarely sweet voice and as he sang his whole being radiated uplifted joy.

The disciple Sasi said: "Ramakrishna could read the true nature of every man. He used to tell us that these eyes were like window sashes;

and as a person looking through a window can see everything in the room, so by looking through the eyes, he could see everything inside a man. Unmasked frankness came to him in certain states of consciousness. When he would come back to his ordinary consciousness he would be much distressed and ask anxiously: 'Have I said anything wrong? Oh! I beg your pardon.' "

He shrank from offending or injuring anything or any one. Even the bend of a blade of grass under a heavy tread or the breaking of a twig from a tree hurt him and he would give a cry of pain. Once he was at the house of a rich man in Calcutta with one of his disciples for some feast. Thinking him to be an ordinary poor *Sadhu*, no one offered him food or took any notice of him. Seeing his Master thus disregarded, the disciple Rakhal grew indignant and said: "Come, let us go away from this house. Do not let us stay any longer." "No, No," Sri Ramakrishna replied gently. "I must eat something. Ask for food." The servants brought nothing but plain rice. Sri Ramakrishna ate a little of it, then went away. "If I had taken nothing there," he explained to Rakhal, "it might have been very terrible for them."

"Christ's teaching, If a man strike you on one cheek, turn to him the other, our Master perfectly exemplified," the disciple Sasi declared. "If he went to a house where people insulted him, he would bless them and come away. Those who would not bow before any man, he would bow low before them and despite themselves they would have to bend a little."

What impression did Sri Ramakrishna make on those who came in touch with him? These words of the eminent Brahmo leader, Protap Mazumdar, describe it vividly and carry special weight because the one who wrote them is known not only in the East but also in the West, having delivered a course of lectures at the Lowell Institute of Boston and spoken in numerous churches throughout the United States and in England.

"My mind is still floating in the luminous atmosphere which that wonderful man diffuses around him whenever and wherever he goes," Mazumdar writes. "My mind is not yet disenchanted of the mysterious and indefinable pathos which he pours into it whenever he meets me. What is there in common between him and me? I, a Europeanized, civilized, self-centered, semi-skeptical, so-called educated reasoner; and he a poor, illiterate, unpolished, half-idolatrous, friendless Hindu devotee? Why should I sit long hours to attend to him, I who have listened to Disraeli and Fawcett, Stanley and Max Muller, and whole hosts of European scholars and divines?

"I who am an ardent disciple and follower of Christ, a friend and admirer of liberal-minded Christian missionaries and preachers, a devoted adherent and worker of the rationalistic Brahmo

Samaj—why should I be spellbound to hear him? And it is not I only, but dozens like me who do the same. He has been interviewed and examined by many, crowds pour in to visit and talk with him. Some of our clever intellectual fools have found nothing in him. I have weighed their objections well, and what I write now I write deliberately.

"The Hindu saint is a man under forty. He is a Brahmin by caste, he is well-formed in body naturally, but the dreadful austerities through which his character has developed appear to have disordered his system. Yet, in the midst of this emaciation his face retains a fullness, a child-like tenderness, a profound visible humbleness and unspeakable sweetness of expression and a smile that I have seen on no other face that I can remember.

"A Hindu saint is always particular about his externals. He wears the *Gerua* cloth, eats according to strict forms, refuses to have intercourse with men, and is a rigid observer of caste. He is proud and professes secret wisdom. He is always a *Guruji*, a universal counsellor. This man is singularly devoid of such claims. His dress and diet do not differ from those of men except in the general negligence he shows towards both; and as to caste, he openly breaks it every day. He most vehemently repudiates the title of *Guru* or teacher, he shows impatient displeasure at any exceptional honor which people try to pay him, and emphatically disclaims the knowledge of secrets and mysteries. He protests against being lionized, and openly shows his strong dislike to be visited and praised by the curious."

A visitor at the Temple once said to Sri Ramakrishna: "Powhari Baba has a picture of you in his room." Sri Ramakrishna rejoined, pointing to his body: "A pillow-case! Nothing but a pillow-case!" In referring to the inherent modesty of the Master and his detachment from all that might foster vanity or self-importance, the disciple Sasi exclaimed: "What a character and life were his! Without learning, poor and obscure, with little of what the civilized man regards as essential to success, yet how much he did for the world! What marks a civilized man? To be highly educated, to be rich, to be well-dressed. But the lesson he came to teach was that these are secondary; that a civilization based on sense-pleasure, material possessions and acquisition must be always false and hollow; that the real benefactor of mankind is he who leads a holy life in conformity with the highest standards, and who possesses, not worldly wealth, but wisdom."

Socrates taught the same and Plato and the Vedic seers. Sri Ramakrishna once declared in defining such world benefactors: "The Divine sages and great spiritual teachers form, as it were, the inner circle of God's nearest relatives. They are like friends, companions, kinsmen of God.

"Rain, falling upon the roof of a house, flows down to the ground through pipes shaped at the end like the head of a tiger or a bull, so that the water appears to come out of a tiger's mouth, but in reality it descends from the sky; even so the eternal truths that come out of the mouths of these illumined ones are not uttered by those men themselves, but in reality descend from the kingdom of heaven.

"Sunlight is one and the same wherever it falls, but only bright surfaces like clear water, mirrors and polished metals can reflect it fully. So is the Light Divine. It falls equally and impartially on all hearts, but only the pure and clean hearts of the good and holy ones can fully reflect it."

With this picture let this narrative close. The picture was drawn without thought of self-description; but no other could outline more perfectly the exalted beauty of Sri Ramakrishna's character, the benign blessing of his teaching and the greater lesson of his life.

GLOSSARY

GLOSSARY

ACHARYA	Teacher.
ADWAITA	Monism.
AMALAKI	A fruit.
ANTAR-ANGA	Vital organ.
BHAIRAVI	A woman renouncer.
BHAJANA	Service of song.
BHAKTA	A devotee.
BHAKTI	Devotion.
BRAHMACHARYA	First stage of the spiritual life. Literally student life.
CHILUM	A pipe.
DAL	Vegetable pulses.
DHOTI	Chief garment worn by Indian men.
DURGA-PUJA	Festival of the protecting Mother of the Universe.
GERUA	Sannyasin color.
GHAT	Landing.
GHEE	Clarified butter.
GUNAS	Qualities.
GURU	Spiritual teacher.
HARI	A name of the Lord.
JAPAM	Repetition of a holy name or word.
MANDAPAM	Open Temple or pavilion.
MANTRAM	Sacred text or word.
MATH	A monastery or religious centre.
MUKTI	Liberation.
NIRVIKALPA SAMADHI	Seedless superconscious vision.
NITYASIDDHA	One who is born perfect.
PANDIT	Scholar.

PARAMAHAMSA	Illumined soul.
PAYASAM	Gruel.
PRANAYAMA	Breath control.
PRASAD	Blessed food.
PREMA	Supreme devotion.
PURDAH	A curtain.
RAJASIKA	Excessively active.
RUPEE	Indian coin, normal value thirty-two cents.
SADHANA	Spiritual practice.
SADHU	A sage or holy man.
SAMADHI	State of superconscious vision.
SANNYAS	Life of renunciation.
SANNYASIN	A man who has taken up the life of renunciation.
SANNYASINI	A woman who has taken up the life of renunciation.
SANKIRTAN	Service of song.
SARI	Chief garment worn by Indian women.
SAT-CHIT-ANANDAM	Existence, knowledge, bliss absolute.
SHRADDHA	Memorial service.
SUKSHMA SARIRA	Subtle body.
TANTRIKAS	Worshippers of Divine Mother.
TOL	A school.
TULASI	A sacred plant.
UPADESHAM	The holy word given by the spiritual teacher.
VAIRAGYAM	Renunciation or non-attachment.
VIDYA	Knowledge.
ZEMINDAR	A large landholder like a count.

BOYHOOD AND RELIGIOUS NAMES OF DISCIPLES

NARENDRA	Swami Vivekananda
RAKHAL	Swami Brahmananda
LATU	Swami Adbhutananda
GOPALDADA	Swami Advaitananda
BABURAM	Swami Premananda
NIRANJAN	Swami Niranjanananda
YOGIN	Swami Yogananda
SASI	Swami Ramakrishnananda
SARAT	Swami Saradananda
GANGADHAR	Swami Akhandananda
TARAK	Swami Shivananda
KALI	Swami Abhedananda
SUBODH	Swami Subodhananda
TULASI	Swami Nirmalananda
SARADA	Swami Trigunatitananda
HARIPRASANNA	Swami Vijnanananda

ADVERTISEMENTS

WORKS BY SWAMI PARAMANANDA

	FLEXIBLE	CLOTH
Rhythm of Life—Poems	$2.00	$1.50
The Vigil—Poems	2.00	1.50
Soul's Secret Door—Poems	2.00	1.50
Book of Daily Thoughts and Prayers	2.50	......
The Path of Devotion		1.25
La Voie de la Devotion (French Translation)		1.25
The Way of Peace and Blessedness		1.25
Vedanta in Practice		1.00
Reincarnation and Immortality		1.00

PRACTICAL SERIES

Concentration and Meditation	.75
Faith as a Constructive Force	.75
Self-Mastery	.75
Creative Power of Silence	.75
Spiritual Healing	.75
Secret of Right Activity	.75

Full Set $4.00. Postage Extra

COMPARATIVE STUDY SERIES

Emerson and Vedanta	1.00
Christ and Oriental Ideals	1.25
Plato and Vedic Idealism	1.25

BOOKLETS AND PAMPHLETS

Problem of Life and Death	.35
Universal Ideal of Religion	.25
Power of Thought	.25
Principles and Purpose of Vedanta	.25
Science and Practice of Yoga	.20
Yoga and Christian Mystics	.20
Civilization and Spiritualization	.10

Postage Extra on All Books Listed

TRANSLATIONS FROM THE SANSKRIT BY SWAMI PARAMANANDA

BHAGAVAD-GITA (3rd Edition). Attractive pocket size. Flexible binding, $1.50. Plain cloth, $1.25. Postage 8 cents.

THE UPANISHADS. With commentary. Vol. I (2nd Edition). Blue cloth, gold lettering, $1.50. Plain cloth, $1.25. Postage 10 cents.

WORKS BY SISTER DEVAMATA

DAYS IN AN INDIAN MONASTERY	$3.00
SRI RAMAKRISHNA AND HIS DISCIPLES	2.50
BUILDING OF CHARACTER (Ready for Press)	2.00
WHAT IS DEATH? (Ready for Press)	2.00

BOOKLETS

THE PRACTICE OF DEVOTION	.25
THE INDIAN MIND AND INDIAN CULTURE	.20
SLEEP AND SAMADHI	.20
ROBERT BROWNING AND THE VEDANTA	.20
DEVELOPMENT OF THE WILL	.20
WHAT IS MAYA?	.20
HEALTH AND HEALING	.30

COMPILED BY SISTER DEVAMATA

SAYINGS AND PARABLES OF SRI RAMAKRISHNA	2.00

POSTAGE EXTRA ON ALL BOOKS LISTED

DAYS IN AN INDIAN MONASTERY

BY SISTER DEVAMATA

344 Pages; 10 Illustrations

Fabrikoid and Cloth Binding, $3.00. Postage Extra

CONTENTS: Foreword; Introduction; I—Monastic Life in India; II—A Great Indian Monk; III—Arrival at Madras; IV—Life at the Monastery; V—Temple Festivals; VI—Spiritual Practice and Religious Observances; VII—Forest Schools of Ancient India; VIII—Indian Education of Today; IX—Building a New Monastery at Bangalore; X—The Head of the Order; XI—Public Meetings, the Indian Theatre and Indian Music; XII—Social Ceremonies and Entertainments; XIII—The Indian Woman and the Indian Home; XIV—A Woman Saint of India; XV—The Presence in the Temple on the Ganges; XVI—Disciples of a Great Master; XVII—At Calcutta; XVIII—The Poor of India; XIX—The True Significance of Caste; XX—Eastern and Western Religious Ideals.

PRESS NOTICES

From Sister Devamata's wide experience have come other books, and several booklets, concerning the Indians, their religion and ideals, but perhaps none more illuminative of their life, both spiritual and secular, than this record of her days in an Indian monastery. . . . But the book deals not wholly with the religious aspect of India. Pictures of the Indian women and their home life, of social ceremonies and entertainments, of the theatres and music, and a chapter on the true significance of caste are equally informative and interesting. . . . The book is written with a clarity of vision that is impressive.—*The Transcript, Boston, Mass.*

While "Days in an Indian Monastery" is in no sense a reply to "Mother India," there is so much light shed, incidentally, on the social life of India that in a measure it may be said to refute largely what Katherine Mayo has recorded. . . . If it is in the hope of creating a wider understanding and deeper sense of kinship between East and West that she offers her reminiscences, it should be said at the outset that she has fully accomplished her purpose, for her observations are eminently enlightening, her style vivid and her viewpoint at all times sympathetic. . . . Interesting as are the chapters portraying the monastic life in India, to the lay mind those describing the social ceremonies and entertainments are fully as absorbing. . . . Of Indian music many interesting observations are adduced. . . . What is written makes the student who has read "Mother India" hesitate to accept Miss Mayo's conclusions as revelatory of the country by and large. . . . Sister Devamata . . . has done a great service to the Indian people by interpreting them through her clear-seeing eyes, to the West. Her book should reach a wide circle of readers.—*Sam T. Clover, Saturday Night, Los Angeles, Calif.*

. . . Sister Devamata's offering of "Days in an Indian Monastery" comes like a fragrant breeze from the Orient to those who are willing to investigate both sides of a subject. . . . Devamata presents a comprehensive view of India from various aspects. . . . Having lived in India for some time it may be inferred that the author knows something about her subject. The fact that she sees the need for certain reforms in India, yet still holds India aloft as a spiritual beacon light to the world, speaks well for her unprejudiced, discriminating mind and for India's ideals.—*James Warnack, The Times, Los Angeles, Calif.*

. . . Sister Devamata . . . lived for a long period in a cloister in a suburb of Madras, where she devoted herself to religious studies. Here she came in touch with many of the greatest Indian teachers and philosophers and had the unusual opportunity, denied to most Westerners, of gaining entrance into high caste Brahmin families and making observations. Sister Devamata is a careful observer and draws exquisite pen pictures. Her delineations are vivid and true to life and they hold the interest of the reader from beginning to end. The book, which is both instructive and entertaining, is enlightening and ought to clear up many misconceptions.—*The Westliche Post, St. Louis, Missouri.*

. . . Sister Devamata dips into the history and life of India and brings forth colorful descriptions of both the ancient Indo-Aryan civilization and the India of more recent times. . . . Remarkably vivid is "Spiritual Practices and Religious Observances," revealed in charming literary style. . . . Sister Devamata is widely experienced in European life and ably draws illuminating parallels between the social usages and customs of Europe and Asia. She lived long among the Hindus and shared freely in their outer and inner life.—*The Star-News, Pasadena, Calif.*